IMAGES OF WAR

NARVIK AND THE NORWEGIAN CAMPAIGN 1940

RARE PHOTOGRAPHS FROM WARTIME ARCHIVES

PHILIP JOWETT

Pen & Sword
MILITARY

First published in Great Britain in 2022 by
PEN & SWORD MILITARY
an imprint of Pen & Sword Books Ltd
Yorkshire – Philadelphia

Copyright © Philip Jowett, 2022

ISBN 978-1-52679-654-7

The right of Philip Jowett to be identified as the author of this work has been asserted by him in accordance with the Copyright, Designs and Patents Act 1988.

A CIP catalogue record for this book is available from the British Library.

All rights reserved. No part of this book may be reproduced or transmitted in any form or by any means, electronic or mechanical including photocopying, recording or by any information storage and retrieval system, without permission from the Publisher in writing.

Typeset by Concept, Huddersfield, West Yorkshire, HD4 5JL.
Printed and bound in England by CPI Group (UK) Ltd, Croydon CR0 4YY.

Pen & Sword Books Ltd incorporates the Imprints of Aviation, Atlas, Family History, Fiction, Maritime, Military, Discovery, Politics, History, Archaeology, Select, Wharncliffe Local History, Wharncliffe True Crime, Military Classics, Wharncliffe Transport, Leo Cooper, The Praetorian Press, Remember When, White Owl, Seaforth Publishing and Frontline Books.

For a complete list of Pen & Sword titles please contact
PEN & SWORD BOOKS LTD
47 Church Street, Barnsley, South Yorkshire, S70 2AS, England
E-mail: enquiries@pen-and-sword.co.uk
Website: www.pen-and-sword.co.uk
or
PEN & SWORD BOOKS
1950 Lawrence Rd, Havertown, PA 19083, USA
E-mail: uspen-and-sword@casematepublishers.com
Website: www.penandswordbooks.com

Contents

Introduction 1

Chapter One
Defending Neutrality 3

Chapter Two
The Build-up to Invasion 25

Chapter Three
The Fall of Denmark: Operation 'Weserubung Sud' 37

Chapter Four
The German Invasion of Norway 49

Chapter Five
The Narvik Sea Battles, 10–13 April 77

Chapter Six
The Germans Advance 91

Chapter Seven
The Allies Arrive in Norway 113

Chapter Eight
Lillehammer 127

Chapter Nine
Air Warfare over Norway 137

Chapter Ten
Allied Failures in Central Norway 153

Chapter Eleven
The Fighting in Northern Norway, 8 May–1 June **167**

Chapter Twelve
The Allied Evacuation from Central Norway **181**

Chapter Thirteen
The Battle for Narvik, 14 April–28 May **195**

Chapter Fourteen
The End of the Norwegian Campaign **221**

Dedication

This book is respectfully dedicated to Peter Abbott (1933–2020), who was one of several military historians who helped me in my early writing career. Peter was a highly dedicated and respected student of military history and an avid researcher into lesser known military subjects. He had a file on just about any military subject of the twentieth century and was a first call when it came to requests for information. Most of his researches from the 1960s until the early 2000s were undertaken in the days before the internet. The groundwork laid by Peter and other historians was vital to the study of military history over the last fifty years. This early research laid the ground for a new generation of historians to expand and share their knowledge with the help of modern technology.

Introduction

After the unprovoked German invasion of Poland in September 1939 and the declaration of war by the Franco-British alliance, an eight-month 'Phoney War' ensued. There was limited ground warfare during the last few months of 1939 along the German-French border, although the French army did launch an offensive into German Saarland between 7 and 16 September. After the French withdrew, the rest of the year and early 1940 saw only limited skirmishes along the border. The war at sea and in the air between the Germans and Allies continued but the world's attention was distracted by fighting between the USSR and Finland. This was the so-called 'Winter War', which lasted from November 1939 until March 1940 and almost involved French and British troops on the Finnish side. Although in the end there was no intervention by the Allies, their attention was now drawn to the strategic importance of Scandinavia. No one had any doubt that 1940 would see a much more serious stage of the conflict and that production of new ships, tanks and planes would be vital. Iron ore and oil would be important for all the warring nations and there were only a few sources for them. Romania and the Soviet Union supplied Germany with most of its oil in 1940, while Sweden was its main supplier of iron ore. As part of their strategic war planning, the Franco-British high commands believed that one way to damage the German war plans was to cut off their supplies of iron ore. Although the iron ore came from Swedish mines, it had to be sent to Germany via the northern Norwegian ice-free port of Narvik. This port now took on great strategic importance as its control would guarantee or interdict the supply of iron ore. Both Britain and France were worried about the growth of the German armed forces and the possibility that an offensive would be launched in the west in 1940.

Hitler's attitude towards Norway was affected by a visit from a former Norwegian defence minister. On 14 December 1939 the Norwegian right-wing politician Vidkun Quisling had an audience with Adolf Hitler, during which the experienced and astute Quisling proved to be very persuasive in talking Hitler round to the idea of invading Norway. Quisling gave Hitler his strong opinion that not only the Allies but also the Soviet Union might potentially invade Norway. This, Quisling explained, would stop the supply of iron ore to Germany and curtail Hitler's plans to build more military hardware. Hitler was interested enough in Quisling's information to instruct Admiral

Raeder, the commander-in-chief of the Kriegsmarine, to produce a document named 'Studie Nord' to assess the feasibility of an invasion of Norway. The study recommended that German landings should take place along the Norwegian coast from Oslo to Tromsø. It said that the conquest of Norway would be vital for the proposed 'Siege of Britain' that was in Hitler's long-term plan.

On the Allied side the invasion of Norway was discussed at length as a way of taking the war to Germany. Although led by the British command, support for the idea was received from the French military and political leadership, who had their own reason for favouring an intervention in Scandinavia as it could delay the German plans to attack France in the spring of 1940. As early as 29 September 1939 the First Lord of the Admiralty, Winston Churchill, had suggested a plan to lay mines off the Norwegian coast.

Advanced plans to lay a minefield off the Norwegian coast to block Port Lulea close to Narvik were seriously discussed on 5 April. There were deep concerns about an Allied infringement of Norwegian neutrality and the worldwide condemnation that it would bring. As both sides considered their next move it became obvious that it was a matter of when not if Norway would become a battleground for the Germans and Allies.

Chapter One

Defending Neutrality

During the 1930s Denmark, Norway and Sweden were determined to remain neutral in the event of a world conflict. They had no wish to be involved in a war between Europe's major powers and largely kept out of global political arguments. Like most other nations, the three countries' economies had been severely affected by the worldwide depression of the 1920s and 1930s. Sweden had a large and reasonably well equipped army, navy and air force, and its economy was much larger than those of the other two countries. Denmark and Norway had spent the first forty years of the twentieth century reducing their military capabilities. They may have been determined to defend their neutrality by force but financial cuts to their military budgets made this difficult, if not impossible.

The Danish military high command, under their commander-in-chief Lieutenant General William Wain Prior, were well aware of the weakness of their army. By the late 1930s the Danish standing army had a strength of 35,000 troops, which would rise to 55,000 when the reservists were mobilised in 1939. This relatively large force could not be sustained and in the winter of that year about 40,000 troops were sent home on leave. The Danish Army in April 1940 had an actual strength of between 14,000 and 14,500 men, with up to 8,000 of them recently drafted. Some had been recruited at the most eight weeks before the invasion and had only the most rudimentary training. They were organised into the Zealand and Jutland Divisions and the garrison of Bornholm. The Danes had a small armoured force comprising three Swedish-made Pansarbil M/39 armoured cars. These had been developed for the Danes in 1937 and the first three had been delivered, with another fifteen on order not arriving before the war began. In addition they had two older Swedish Landsverk L-180 armoured cars that had been ordered in 1935 and delivered in 1937. They were reported to have bought single examples of the Italian Fiat 3000 light tank, a French NC2 light tank and a British Carden-Lloyd 'patrol' light tank. There were a small number of Nimbus motorcycles with sidecars fitted with the effective Madsen 20mm anti-aircraft/anti-tank gun. Artillery used by the Danes were the Krupp-designed M02 (75mm) and Schneider 105mm M30, plus a few 150mm howitzers, either Schneider or Bofors. Other guns included twenty-four 37mm anti-tank guns, twelve Vickers 75mm M32 anti-aircraft guns and ninety-six mortars.

The Danish Air Forces had four squadrons divided between the Army Air Force and the Naval Air Service, with a total of forty-eight to fifty planes. Naval Air Service aircraft comprised a squadron of British Hawker Nimrod fighters. Army Air Force aircraft had consisted of British Gloster Gauntlet fighters, but these were being replaced by fairly modern Dutch Fokker XXI fighter planes. Attempts to buy or build under licence more modern aircraft came to nothing due to the outbreak of war in 1939. The Danes had hoped to licence-produce copies of the Dutch Fokker G1A twin boomed fighter and the British Fairy Battle light bomber. The Danish navy was fairly large, with two coastal defence ships, three minelayers, nine minesweepers, seven submarines and six torpedo boats. This force gave up without a fight allowing a German troopship to land troops at Copenhagen harbour unopposed.

The Norwegian armed forces were on paper larger than those of their neighbours to the south but they suffered from most of the same weaknesses in equipment and training. The official mobilisation strength of the army was 90,000 but on 9 April 1940 only 19,000 men were under arms. Norway chose partial mobilisation even under threat of war, and even then the recruits were informed by letter that they needed to attend barracks! The main formations of the Norwegian Army in 1940 were six army divisions that were only divisions in name. In reality, a Norwegian division was an administrative command whose role was to act as a training organisation. There were divisions based at the cities of Halden, Oslo, Bergen, Trondheim, Harstad and Kristiansand. Each division had a brigade as its main component unit, with each brigade having two regiments made up of two battalions of infantry each. All six divisions had in addition an artillery regiment, with the 1st, 2nd and 5th Divisions having field artillery and the 3rd, 4th and 6th Divisions having mountain artillery.

They also had small support units on their strength including engineers, signals and communications. The 1st, 2nd and 5th Divisions also had cavalry regiments: the 1st, 2nd and 3rd Dragoon Regiments. Based at the 1st Regiment's barracks was the single Norwegian tank, which was under development when the war began. There were also a handful of homemade armoured cars which were sufficient for manoeuvres but would be useless against German tanks. Field manoeuvres by the Norwegian Army had been cancelled for several years due to the high cost of organising them. Other cost-cutting measures involved the retaining of the obsolete Krag-Jorgensen M1894 rifle and the continued use of out-of-date 75mm field guns. Unlike nearly every other army of the 1930s the Norwegians chose not to adopt any sub-machine guns because of their cost. Apart from shortages of modern weaponry and equipment, the Norwegian Army had other weaknesses. These included the shortened training period that Norwegian troops received during the 1930s. In 1930 the training period for Norwegian troops was only forty-eight days but by 1939 this had been thankfully extended to eighty-four days. Another weakness was the army's lack of a viable non-commissioned officer rank to bridge the gap between privates and officers. Until the 1930s the Norwegian Army, like most other armies, did have an NCO corps with the ranks of korporal, sersjant, oversersjant, furer and fanejunker. However, Norwegian NCOs complained that although they did the same work as officers, they were regarded as second-class soldiers. Norway in the 1930s was run by politically liberal governments which agreed that some soldiers were spending their whole careers as officers while others could not rise through the ranks. Their solution to this inherent unfairness was to abolish the NCO system, which resulted in a weakening of the Norwegian command structure.

The Norwegian navy, under the command of Admiral H.E. Diesen, was equipped only to defend the country's coastline. Its two biggest ships were the coastal defence ships *Eidsvold*, launched in 1899, and *Norge*, launched in 1900. These ships had 21cm guns in single turrets fore and aft and secondary armament of six 15cm and eight 76mm guns. There were also seven small destroyers (four of which were modern vessels with three 4 inch guns and one 40mm gun), eight minesweepers, ten mine-layers, nine patrol boats and seventeen torpedo boats of First World War vintage. In addition there were nine small coastal submarines which were only capable of operating along the Norwegian coastline. In September 1939, because of the threat of attacks on Norway's neutrality, the Norwegian navy was mobilised (apart from two ships) to defend its territorial waters.

The Norwegian Army Air Service and Naval Air Service were also called up to help defend the country's neutrality. In the early weeks of the war aircraft from all the belligerents were guilty of violating Norwegian air space. The Naval Service had four Italian Breda Ba28 trainers fitted with floats and six Heinkel 115 seaplanes. By far the most numerous aircraft in Norwegian Army Air Force service were the twenty-seven Fokker CVD and twenty Fokker CVE light bombers, but both types were outdated and too slow to compete with German aircraft. The most modern fighters in Norwegian service were the six British Gloster Gladiators which were supposed to replace the six Armstrong-Whitworth AW35s. They also had four Italian Caproni Ca310 bombers which had been acquired in 1939 in a deal which involved large amounts of 'dried and salted cod' – Klippfisk! However, these modern planes turned out to have a poor performance, to the great disappointment of the Norwegians.

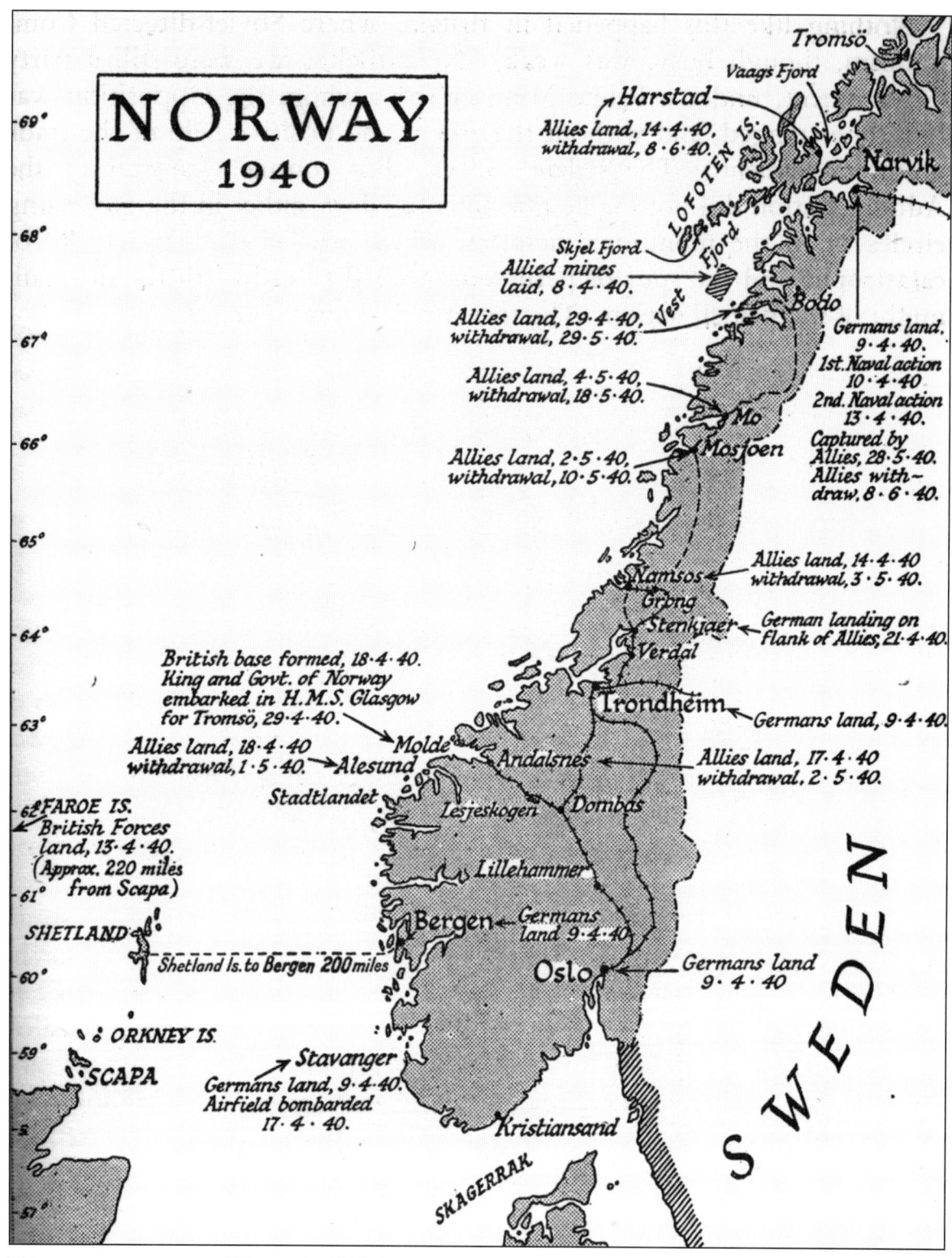

This contemporary map of Norway in 1940 shows the dates of landings and evacuations along the country's coast.

The 70-year-old King Christian X of Denmark takes his daily ride through Copenhagen, reinforcing his image as a people's monarch. Christian had ruled since 1912 and was put in an impossible position when the Germans invaded; unlike his brother King Haakon VII of Norway, he did not encourage any resistance by the Danes. The German invasion was so overwhelming that it was resisted only in a few places along the border and at the royal palace. (Author's Collection)

The crew of a 75mm Danish anti-aircraft gun take part in a practice drill in the weeks before the German invasion in April 1940. They wear the M23 steel helmet with their black greatcoats that dated back to the 1860s and their uniform trousers are rolled up at the bottom. Danish industry produced a number of good weapons, including anti-tank guns and the popular Madsen light machine gun. Their products sold widely on the world arms market in the 1920s and 1930s, although their own small army could never buy them in large quantities. (*Author's Collection*)

Three reserve soldiers pictured in September 1939 with the caption saying that they are more than ready to 'Defend their country's Neutrality'. The size of the Danish Army was totally inadequate to defend the country and Denmark relied totally on the good will of Germany. Although they received assurances that their neutrality would be respected, the behaviour of the Germans in 1938 and 1939 in Czechoslovakia and Poland did not bode well. (*Author's Collection*)

Danish anti-aircraft gunners fold out the legs of their Vickers 75mm M32 anti-aircraft gun on 17 December 1939. There were only twelve of these modern guns in service with the Danish Army in April 1940. This gun's eleven-man crew are wearing the 1864 black greatcoat along with more up-to-date khaki side caps. (*Author's Collection*)

Danish troops take part in a pre-war exercise wearing their mix of nineteenth- and twentieth-century uniforms. The distinctive steel helmet was fairly modern, having been introduced in 1923, and their stone-grey tunics and trousers were introduced in the same year. Their outdated black coats dated back to 1864 and their trench shovels had been issued in 1870. Gas masks were a relatively new item of equipment, having been introduced in 1926, and the Madsen light machine gun carried by one of the soldiers was a twentieth-century weapon. (*Author's Collection*)

A horse artillery unit of the Danish Army move their 7.5cm Felkanon M02 field gun forward during a field exercise in the build-up to the Second World War. The Danish Army had ninety-six of these medium artillery pieces in service in 1939 but few if any were brought into action in 1940. (*Author's Collection*)

Another horse artillery unit brings its 7.5cm gun into action in preparation to meet the threat of a violation of its neutrality. Denmark's artillery included the already mentioned ninety-six 7.5cm field guns, and there were also forty-eight 10.5cm Felkanon M30 and thirty-two 15cm guns but these were made up of three models, with twenty-four M29s, four M23s and four M17s. (*Author's Collection*)

A Fokker CV of the Danish Air Force is pictured in the build-up to the outbreak of the Second World War. The Danes maintained very limited air defences and hoped that their neutrality would ensure that they never had to defend their country. The Fokker was outdated by 1940 and if any had managed to get airborne they would have been quickly dealt with by the Luftwaffe. One did take off on 9 April but was shot down by the planes attacking Vaerløse airfield. (*Author's Collection*)

A Royal Danish Navy Aviation pilot – 'Marinens Flyvevaesen' – poses with his parachute before going out on a flight in 1939. His plane is a British-made Hawker Nimrod, which was the naval version of the classic Hawker Fury fighter. The Nimrod was first introduced in 1933 and two examples were sent to the Danes in the same year. Another ten Nimrods were built locally under licence before 1935 and eight were still in service in April 1940. (*Author's Collection*)

One of a handful of Fokker D.XIII fighters on the strength of the Danish Air Force is seen being prepared for a flight before the 1940 war. Although still a front-line fighter with the Dutch and Finnish, the D.XIII was never going to be a match for the German Me109. The Danes ordered two D.XXIs which arrived in 1938 and a total of ten were built during 1939 and early 1940. (*Author's Collection*)

The HDMS *Niels Juel* coastal defence ship was one of the largest ships in the Royal Danish Navy and was constructed over a four-year period from 1914 to 1918. It was not finally commissioned until 1923 largely due to the constraints of the First World War even though Denmark remained neutral. The ship was armed with ten 150mm guns and two 57mm anti-aircraft guns and had been extensively modernised in the 1930s. Like the rest of the Danish Navy, *Niels Juel* did not take part in the brief campaign of April 1940. (*Author's Collection*)

King Haakon VII had reigned on the Norwegian throne since 1905 but was Danish by birth, having previously been known as Prince Carl of Denmark. He had served in the Royal Danish Navy and when the union of Sweden and Norway was dissolved in 1905 he was offered the throne of Norway. He was a popular monarch and his refusal to accept the *fait-accompli* offered by the Germans in 1940 increased that popularity. During his exile in England he refused to abdicate, and returned to Norway in June 1945 where he continued to reign until his death in 1957. (*Author's Collection*)

Crown Prince Olaf inspecting Norwegian Air Force pilots. Overhead fly three Fokker CVD light bombers which, along with the slightly improved CVE, made up the vast majority of aircraft in Norwegian service. When the Germans invaded in April 1940 the Crown Prince backed his father's decision to support continued resistance by their armed forces. (*Author's Collection*)

A Norwegian soldier models the uniform of the army worn with the Norwegian M1931 steel helmet with an oval badge with the lion of Norway embossed on the front. This helmet was based on the Swedish civil defence helmet and saw limited service during the 1940 campaign. The rest of his uniform is standard M1912 model made from grey-green cloth and was worn with a sheepskin coat in winter when available. (*Author's Collection*)

(**Opposite, above**) These two home-made armoured cars pictured during a pre-war exercise sum up the armoured force that the Norwegians could put into the field in 1940. Other than a few such improvised vehicles, they had a single light tank armed with a machine gun, which was given the rather grand title of 'the National Tank'. The Danish and Norwegian armed forces were heavily constrained by the low defence budgets that their respective governments allowed them in the 1930s. (*Author's Collection*)

(**Opposite, below**) The crew of a Norwegian-made 7.5cm L/45 M32 anti-aircraft gun going through their drill before the war. This gun had been in service since 1936. When the war began four of them were positioned at Raufoss, but two of these were sent to Elverum to protect the king and his government. Oslo was protected by four batteries of these guns with three guns per battery, and during the war they were reported to have shot down at least one German bomber. (*Author's Collection*)

One of the three Norwegian dragoon regiments ride out on an exercise with one of their *Hjulryttere* ('Wheel Riders') keeping up on his bicycle. During the Norwegian invasion some dragoons did use their horses but they also used bicycles and skis to move around. The dragoons wear a variety of uniforms including kepis and tunics dating back to the nineteenth century. Others wear the British First World War model steel helmet, one of two models in use concurrently with the Norwegian Army. (*Author's Collection*)

Norwegian ski troops during a military exercise in the winter of 1939/1940, at the time of the Winter War between Finland and the Soviet Union. Norway feared an attack by the Russians on their country as an extension of their land grab against Finland. Units were stationed along the Finnish border, including ski troops from the bicycle company of each regiment. In the winter bicycle troops converted to using skis and performed mostly reconnaissance roles. (Author's Collection)

Curious civilians gather around one of their country's six British Gloster Gladiator fighters in the build-up to the German invasion. Like many smaller nations, in the 1930s the Norwegians had ordered aircraft from foreign manufacturers. The outbreak of the war in September 1939 meant that many of these orders were cancelled. This resulted in countries like Norway having to make do with what aircraft they already had to face Nazi aggression. (Author's Collection)

A Norwegian Army Air Service Fokker CVE light bomber with its two-man crew prepares to take off in 1939. The heavy reliance on the outdated CVD aircraft and the slightly improved CVE meant that the Norwegian Air Force had little effect on the campaign in 1940. The CVD had a poor maximum speed limit of 142mph, which rendered any that did take off easy pickings for the Luftwaffe in April 1940. *(Author's Collection)*

During a pre-war night exercise the crew of a Colt-Browning M29 heavy machine gun fire off into the dark forest around them. Both crewmen have full equipment including winter coats and other warm weather clothing carried in their haversacks. The chaotic situation in the Norwegian military in the 1930s was largely due to the constant cuts to the military budget. Although Norway was determined to defend her neutrality, her government was not willing to pay for modern armed forces. *(Author's Collection)*

The Hotchkiss M1914 was the main type of machine gun in service with the Norwegian Army in the 1920s. It was largely replaced by the Norwegian version of the Browning heavy machine gun in the 1930s. Here it is seen on a pre-war exercise with the King's Life Guard who wear their blue uniform with British-pattern steel helmet. (*Author's Collection*)

A Norwegian Army communications unit using a mobile telephone switchboard fastened to a tree trunk during pre-war exercises. During the coming campaign the Norwegians who carried on fighting would rely on this kind of equipment to keep in touch with other units on other fronts. (*Author's Collection*)

(**Opposite, above**) Norwegian ski troops patrolling the wide open spaces of their country in the winter of 1939/1940. The Norwegian winter lasted from December to February and the weather varied greatly from the coast to the rest of the country. Coastal regions are warmed by the Gulf Stream but the interior of the country, especially in the east, is extremely cold during the winter. During the summer Norwegian ski troops usually operated on bicycles as mobile infantry but most were more at home on skis, having learned to ski from a very young age. (*Author's Collection*)

(**Opposite, below**) Two Norwegian mortar teams prepare to fire their Brandt M27 81mm mortars on a pre-war winter exercise in 1939. Most European nations based their mortars on the French Brandt design, which was itself based on the British Stokes mortar of the First World War. In Norway a licence-built variant of the Brandt was given the designation 8.1cm Bombekaster M/35 and came into service alongside the imported mortars. (*Author's Collection*)

(**Above**) Norwegian Red Cross Auxiliary Corps volunteers are seen on parade in the city of Trondheim in the pre-war period. Most countries in Europe maintained a civil defence force in the lead-up to the Second World War. Around the world the fear of gas attacks was constant in the 1930s, with the bitter memory of the brutal events of the First World War still fresh. Countries like Norway that had stayed neutral during that war were still aware of the dangers of gas. They were also aware of the recent displays of mass bombing by the German Condor Legion during the Spanish Civil War. (*Author's Collection*)

(**Opposite, above**) Three Norwegian German-made Heinkel 115 seaplanes of the Naval Air Service fly over a navy minesweeper in a pre-war propaganda photograph. The Norwegian Navy was never intended to be able to take on the battleships and battlecruisers of the major navies. Its ships were mainly small vessels equipped for defending the long Norwegian coastline. (*Author's Collection*)

(**Opposite, below**) Three Norwegian Navy submarines moored at their naval base before the war. Six B-class submarines, B1 to B6, were built under licence at the shipyard at Karljohansvern. Based on the US Navy L-class submarine design, they were built between 1922 and 1929. During the war B2, B4 and B5 were captured by the Germans in April, while B6 surrendered to them in May and B3 was scuttled by her crew in June. B1 escaped to the UK, arriving there on 8 June. (*Author's Collection*)

(**Above**) General Kristian Kristiansen Laake, the 65-year-old commander-in-chief of the Norwegian Army in April 1940, is seen here at his desk. He had served as commander-in-chief in February 1931 and was in full support of the unpopular government policy of reducing the size of the Norwegian Army in the 1930s. Any resistance by Norwegian officers to the drastic cuts was dealt with by Laake, who told them to obey the politicians' instructions. Laake was not a fighting general and was soon replaced by the more resolute Colonel Otto Ruge. Ruge was promoted to the rank of general in order to fulfil his new role, which he continue to do resolutely throughout the Norwegian Campaign. (*Author's Collection*)

Chapter Two

The Build-up to Invasion

In the first week of April 1940 the Germans and the Franco-British Alliance were both preparing for their own intervention in Norway. German plans for an invasion of Scandinavia ran into several major problems, principally the absolute superiority of the Royal Navy over the Kriegsmarine. To counter this Franco-British superiority, the Luftwaffe would commit far more planes to the invasion than the Allies could. Both German and Franco-British intelligence services were aware that the other side were preparing to commit troops to Norway. Hitler's intention to invade Denmark at the same time as Norway was explained by him as a necessary move to protect his forces' rear from any Allied attack. Germany's original rather vague 'Studie Nord' was now redrawn into two separate but concurrent plans: 'Weserubung' ('River Exercise') for Norway and 'Weserubung Sud' ('River Exercise South') for Denmark. The plans were signed off by the German dictator on 2 April and the invasion was to begin the very next day.

Germany's plan depended on surprise but this was to prove difficult because of the large numbers of RAF reconnaissance planes over Norwegian waters. Hitler decided it was essential that his forces should take the initiative. The invasion effectively began on 3 April when transport ships quietly left their ports in northern Germany.

Allied plans were now accelerated, with the war to be taken to Germany by the powerful forces of the Royal Navy. On 4 April the Franco-British military planners ordered sixteen submarines to move into Norwegian waters. The next day the battleship HMS *Renown* set off from the Royal Navy base at Scapa Flow, along with twelve destroyers. A small force of French Navy ships – a cruiser, two destroyers and a submarine – joined the flotilla. The British ships just missed intercepting the German heavy cruiser *Admiral Hipper* on the 6th. By the 7th bad weather had set in across the region, with *Renown* and her escort struggling through heavy snowstorms. One of the destroyers, HMS *Glowworm*, lost touch with the rest of the Royal Navy flotilla when she tried to rescue a crewman who fell overboard. Now isolated, *Glowworm* was soon surrounded by superior Kriegsmarine ships and was sunk after a one-sided but gallant battle on the 8th. Meanwhile the rest of the Royal Navy force had fulfilled its mission to lay mines off the northern coast of Norway. At 7.00am on 8 April the British and French ambassadors informed the Norwegian government that minefields had been laid off their coast during the night. The Norwegians were livid that their neutrality had been infringed but their intelligence sources informed them that a German invasion fleet was on its way. A telephone call from the port of Kristiansand then informed the government that 122 men, including soldiers, had been rescued from the German supply ship *Rio de Janeiro*, which had been sunk by a Royal Navy submarine. Intelligence from Swedish sources had arrived on the 7th saying that fifteen to twenty German ships had left their ports. Another source from Denmark on the 8th warned that large German ships had been seen sailing northwards. These warnings caused no reaction in Norway and mobilisation was not ordered. Both Denmark and Norway chose to depend on their neutrality in the vain hope that the Germans and Allies would not land on their shores.

The German supply ship *Altmark* sheltering in Jossingfjord in Norway, with almost 300 British sailors held below decks. Having infringed Norwegian neutrality by entering her territorial waters, the ship's crew were shocked to be attacked by the crew of HMS *Cossack* on 16 February 1940. First Lord of the Admiralty Winston Churchill ordered that a flotilla of destroyers under Captain Philip Vian should sail to Norway to liberate the captured seamen. After a hand-to-hand struggle the German crew were overwhelmed and were in turn taken prisoner by the *Cossack*'s crew. Both ships had entered neutral territory illegally but the British believed they had right on their side. The German press, however, did not agree and complained about the British infringement of Norway's neutrality! (*Author's Collection*)

Two happy old 'sea dogs' of the British Mercantile Marine photographed after their release from *Altmark* by the crew of HMS *Cossack*. According to press reports, the seamen were crammed below decks in squalid conditions. Although *Cossack* was infringing Norwegian neutrality, the conditions in which the British sailors were being held was seen as justification for the breaking of international law. *(Author's Collection)*

General von Falkenhorst, commander of the 21st Army, who was put in charge of Operation 'Weserubung', is pictured scrutinising a map with General Eduard Dietl. Dietl was in command of the 3rd Mountain Division (*Gerbirgsdivisionen*), one of two divisions earmarked for 'Weserubung'. Both men were aware that Hitler wanted the invasion of Denmark and Norway to be completed as soon as possible. His plans for the offensive on the Western Front must not be affected by the 'side-show' in Scandinavia. Falkenhorst was not known to Hitler but had served in Finland in 1918 and had proved himself during the Polish Campaign in September 1939. *(Author's Collection)*

Vidkun Quisling was a former Norwegian military officer with right-wing sympathies. In the 1920s he served as a diplomat in the Soviet Union, where he saw at first hand the result of a revolutionary government. He became a politician in the early 1930s and served as Minister of Defence under two prime ministers. His 'Nasjonal Samling' ('National Union') political party, which was formed in 1933, was to all intents and purposes the Norwegian Fascist Party. In 1940, having failed to raise the profile of his party, he and his followers assisted the German invasion of their country and from 1942 to 1945 Quisling served as prime minister of a 'puppet' Norwegian government. He was executed in October 1945 for his betrayal of his country. (*Author's Collection*)

German troops assemble at an airfield in northern Germany, ready to take off for the invasion of Norway. The Junkers Ju 52/3m transport plane – one of which is seen in the background – was fundamental to the success of the invasions of Denmark and Norway. This plane, which was developed from a 1930s Lufthansa civil airliner, could carry thirteen paratroopers, or eighteen soldiers and their equipment, or twelve wounded men on stretchers. (*Author's Collection*)

Panzer I light tanks are loaded onto a transport ship days before the invasion of Scandinavia. This tank was to see widespread service during the Blitzkrieg era from 1939 to 1941 and beyond. Because of its light armour and poor armament, the tank was really obsolete by April 1940 but it faced little or no opposition from Allied tanks in Scandinavia. (Author's Collection)

(**Above**) German merchant ships move through an icy sea en route to Norway in April 1940, on the lookout for Royal Navy ships. During the Norwegian Campaign the Germans and Allies continued to ship reinforcements and supplies through the same sea channels. They had to run the gauntlet of enemy surface warships and submarines to get to their destinations, and a number were sunk. (*Author's Collection*)

(**Opposite, above**) A Royal Navy minesweeper sailing towards Norway in the first days of the war at sea around the country. On 8 April a force of Royal Navy destroyers sowed mines off the coast of northern Norway in Vestfjord, close to the port of Bodö, in an attempt to disrupt the transport of iron ore from Narvik by German merchant shipping. The British government only informed the angry Norwegian government about their intention to lay mines after the event. (*Author's Collection*)

(**Opposite, below**) The Royal Navy destroyer HMS *Glowworm* pictured in better days before the Norwegian Campaign. A G-class destroyer built for the Navy in the mid-1930s, she saw service in the arms blockade of Spain during the Civil War of 1936–1939. Her armament was standard for Royal Navy ships of this type with four 4.7-inch main guns, two quadruple torpedo tubes and two quadruple 0.5-inch anti-aircraft guns. Although *Glowworm* was a powerful ship, she was totally outclassed when she faced the might of the German heavy cruiser *Admiral Hipper*. (*Author's Collection*)

H92

(**Above**) HMS *Glowworm* took on a superior force of Kriegsmarine ships in the early hours of 8 April. She had lost touch with the rest of the British force sailing towards Norway after trying to retrieve a crewman who had fallen overboard. She was first confronted by two German destroyers, Z11 and Z18, whose captains called for help, which arrived in the form of the heavy cruiser *Admiral Hipper*. The Royal Navy ship fired torpedoes towards the *Hipper* but the German ship suffered no damage. *Glowworm* was hopelessly outgunned. After being hit by several salvoes from *Hipper*'s guns, her commander, Captain Broadmead-Roope, turned his stricken ship towards the German ship. The much smaller ship rammed the side of *Hipper* and the collision tore off 130ft of the cruiser's armour plating. *Glowworm* then pulled away and turned over in the heavy seas; her boilers then exploded, causing the ship to sink. (*Author's Collection*)

(**Opposite, above**) In the aftermath of the sinking of HMS *Glowworm*, forty British sailors were rescued by the *Admiral Hipper*. Here desperately injured and oil-covered sailors cling to their lifeboat while waiting to be hoisted aboard by the *Hipper*'s crew. The German ship was searching for one of its own crewmen who had fallen overboard during the sea battle. There was still a mutual respect between rival navies at this stage of the war and the *Hipper*'s crew tried to save as many of *Glowworm*'s crew as possible. Captain Broadmead-Roope was not one of the survivors as his frozen hands could no longer grip the rope pulling him to safety. Six of the rescued sailors later died from their wounds and from the large amount of oil they had ingested. Broadmead-Roope was posthumously awarded the Victoria Cross for his courageous command of the ship during the one-sided battle. (*Author's Collection*)

(**Opposite, below**) The Polish Navy submarine *Orzel* (*Eagle*) and her crew had escaped from internment in Estonia after the September 1939 invasion of their homeland. She had been on patrol in the Baltic Sea when the German invasion took place and took shelter in the Baltic state before escaping to Britain in late September. Her services were offered to the British war effort and she was assigned to the Royal Navy's 2nd Submarine Flotilla. On 8 April 1940 *Orzel* sank the clandestine German troop transport *Rio de Janeiro*, killing several hundred troops bound for the invasion of Norway. (*Author's Collection*)

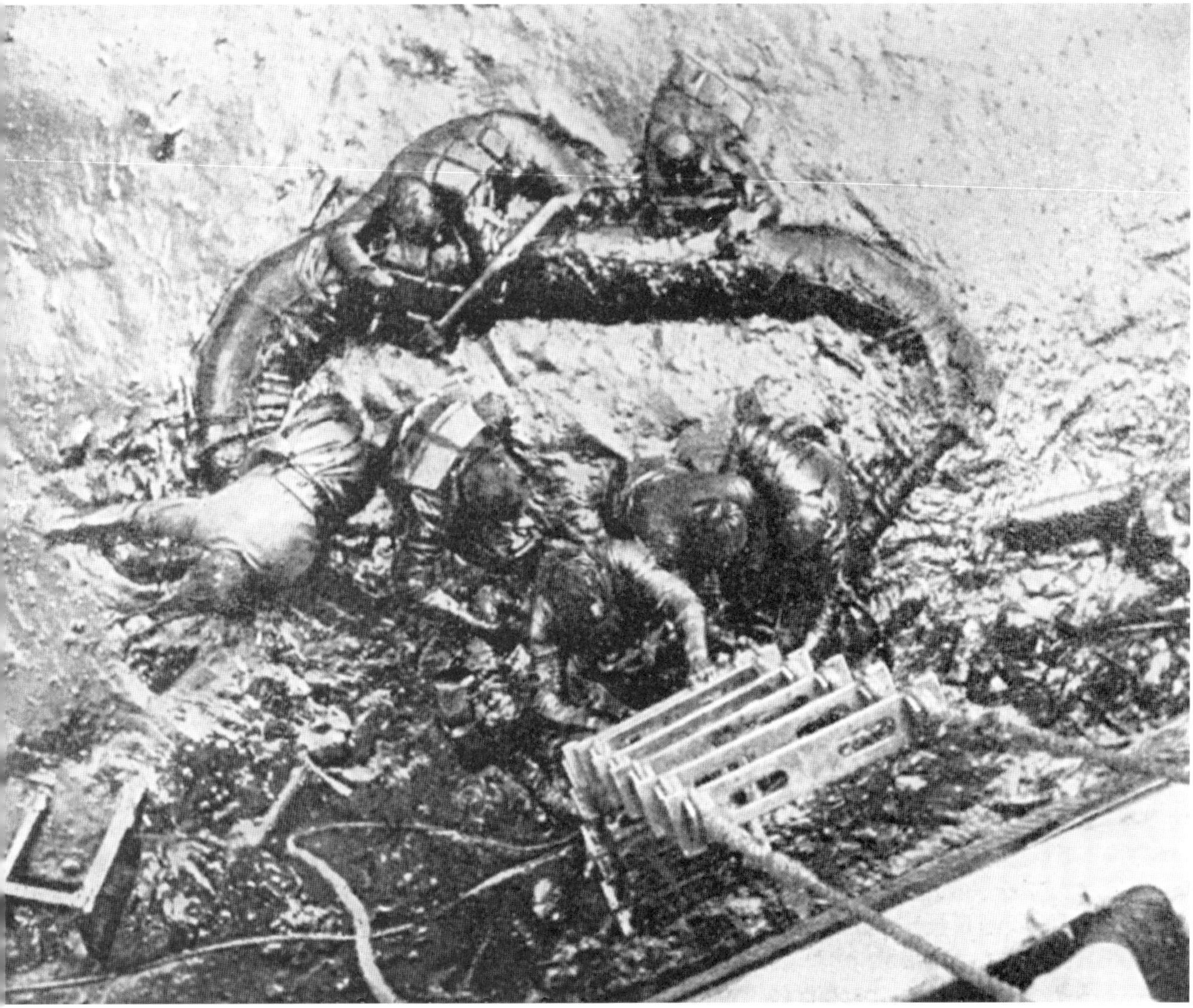

(**Above**) The Royal Navy battlecruiser HMS *Renown*, photographed from a seaplane, clashed with the Kriegsmarine's *Scharnhorst* and *Gneisenau* in the early morning of 9 April. These two powerful German battleships had been escorting a flotilla of destroyers to Norway and were on their way back to their home port at Kiel. When *Renown* spotted the two capital ships her crew realised that her six 15-inch guns were inferior to the combined eighteen 11-inch guns of the German ships. *Renown* fired first but was hit by two German shells before damaging *Gneisenau* with a single 15-inch shell. She also managed to inflict more damage using her lighter 4.5-inch guns to land two shells on the same ship. After a 90-minute engagement the damaged *Gneisenau* and the unscathed *Scharnhorst* used their superior speed to break off the battle and sail for home. *(Author's Collection)*

(**Opposite, below**) The Kriegsmarine cruiser *Karlsruhe* was an early victim of the Norwegian Campaign. She had landed troops at the port of Kristiansand in southern Norway and was on her way home to Germany when she was attacked on 9 April. A torpedo from the submarine HMS *Truant* caused severe damage and *Karlsruhe* was scuttled by her crew, with the *coup de grace* delivered by a German torpedo boat. (*Author's Collection*)

(**Above left**) The crew of HMS *Truant* stand on the deck of their submarine as she arrives back into port after her successful attack on the German cruiser *Karlsruhe*. Her victory was slightly tainted by an unsuccessful attack on a ex-German merchant ship which had already been captured by the Royal Navy, unbeknown to *Truant*'s crew. She also attacked the ex-Norwegian merchant ship *Tropic Sea*, which was in German hands and which also had to be scuttled by her crew. (*Author's Collection*)

(**Above right**) The Royal Navy Swordfish class submarine HMS *Snapper* (39S) returns to port in Britain after a successful cruise in Norwegian waters. She sank several German transport ships, stores carriers and a small oil tanker (*Moonsund*) and had managed to save at least one survivor. *Snapper*'s other victims included two Kriegsmarine minesweepers, H.M. *Behren* and *Carsten Janssen*. *Snapper* had been built in 1933 and went on to have a successful career before being sunk in the Bay of Biscay in February 1941. Submariners were a stoic breed and they were well aware that they could easily become the victim in any encounter with surface ships. (*Author's Collection*)

The Royal Navy submarine HMS *Sunfish* is greeted by crewmen from other ships as she returns to a British port. Her captain, Lieutenant Commander J. Slaughter, was awarded the DSO for sinking four ships off the Norwegian coast. In April *Sunfish* sank two German merchant ships, *Amasis* and *Antares*, and two Q-ships, *Schurbeck* and *Oldenburg*. Q-ships were decoy vessels that masqueraded as merchant ships but were armed with concealed guns to attack any Royal Navy ships that moved in to sink them. (*Author's Collection*)

Chapter Three

The Fall of Denmark: Operation 'Weserubung Sud'

In the early hours of the morning of 9 April 1940 the full might of the German Army and the Luftwaffe was unleashed on Denmark. Although Denmark had signed a non-aggression pact with Nazi Germany in the spring of 1939, the German leader Adolf Hitler regarded the country as being in his 'sphere of influence'. Neither this pact nor Denmark's declared neutrality meant anything to the German dictator. Danish intelligence had found out that the invasion of their country was about to begin on 4 April but few preparations were made to counter the attack.

The German invasion force comprised XXXI Corps under the command of General Kaupisch. It was made up of the 170th and 198th Infantry Divisions, as well as the 11th Schutzen Brigade, and was supported by forty-three tanks, two batteries of artillery and three armoured trains. Strategic points including Denmark's airfields and bridges were captured by small units of paratroopers. Air cover was provided by the X Fliegerkorps which had a total of 527 aircraft – ten times the strength of the Danish Air Force. At 4.15am on the 9th German forces crossed the Danish-German border and rushed across the Jutland Peninsula. By 6.15am the invasion was virtually over and the country was in the hands of the Germans. There was some resistance, notably on the southern border with Germany, and shots were fired in defence of the royal palace at Amalienburg. Although the Danish resistance amounted to little more than a few isolated skirmishes, it should be recorded that some troops were willing to die for their country. At the royal palace at 6.00am guards dressed in their Napoleonic era uniforms with bearskin hats fought the Germans in a brief but ferocious fire-fight. This resulted in the Germans withdrawing for a while and the Royal Guard counting their dead: six men had been killed and twelve wounded during the battle. The Danish commander-in-chief, Lieutenant General William Wane Prior, was unaware of the fighting in Jutland and at the royal palace and expressed his anger at the lack of resistance shown by his troops. King Christian asked him if he thought his troops had fought for long enough and the general said: 'Your Highness, the troops have not fought at all!' Winston Churchill was sympathetic to the dilemma faced by the Danish nation, remarking: 'I could not reproach Denmark if she surrendered to Nazi attack.'

With the Danish capital Copenhagen in German hands, the government was quickly pressured into capitulating. Under the lightweight terms of the German occupation King Christian X was allowed to stay on his throne. A small Danish Army was also allowed to remain in existence as the Germans sought to deal with the population with 'velvet gloves'.

In the months before the outbreak of war a unit of Danish troops takes part in a route march. The men are wearing their M1923 uniforms made from yellow-brown cloth. The Danish Army was armed with 7.92mm Krag-Jorgensen M1898 rifles and M1924 Madsen light machine guns. The equipment used by the Danes had been added to during the 1930s, with backpacks being adopted in 1939. Their entrenching tools dated back to the 1860s and might even have been used in the 1864 war with Prussia, while their water bottles were introduced into service in 1895. (Author's Collection)

A lone Danish soldier looks out for any threat from the German Army along the border with Jutland and northern Germany. The flat terrain of the Jutland Peninsula – which makes up about 70 per cent of Danish territory – was ideal for the Blitzkrieg tactics of the German Army. With too few troops the Danish Army could not defend the 42-mile border and could only hope to put up brief resistance. (*Author's Collection*)

The crew of a Danish medium anti-aircraft gun go through their drill in the days before the German invasion. During the 9 April invasion German paratroopers landed on the Danish airfields at Aalborg. A battalion of air landing troops was also flown into Denmark in Junkers Ju 52 transports and landed at the airfield. The surprise attacks on the country meant that heavy weaponry like this gun were not put into action during the invasion. (*Author's Collection*)

A burned-out Danish Fokker D.XIII fighter on Vaerløse airfield on 9 April, having been destroyed before its pilot could get it into the air. The handful of Dutch-designed fighters were the best that the Danish had in April 1940 but they were largely obsolete. If they had managed to take off they would have been swiftly dealt with by the German Messerschmitt 109-E fighters. Any surviving Danish aircraft were put into store but the D.XIIIs do not appear to have been utilised by the Germans. A number of Fokker CV light bombers were sent to the Eastern Front, serving with a ground support unit, the NSGr. 11, in 1944. *(Author's Collection)*

A Danish motorcycle unit waits at a crossroads at the town of Åbenrå in south-western Denmark on 9 April. Their 'Nimbus' motorcycle and sidecar carries a Madsen M38 20mm anti-aircraft/anti-tank gun. This potent weapon – which could penetrate 42mm of armour – was reported to have destroyed two Panzer I light tanks as well as eleven scout cars during the German invasion. *(Author's Collection)*

This small unit of Danish troops armed with a Madsen light machine gun was to see some of the hardest fighting on 9 April. Of these seven men, two would die in the fighting within a few hours of the start of the German invasion. Rather unfairly, many in the Danish population were angry at the lack of resistance by their army. However, the overwhelming odds faced by the miniscule Danish Army meant that any resistance was not only futile but suicidal. (Author's Collection)

A Leichter Panzerspähwagen Sd.Kfz.221 scout car knocked out at Bredevad on 9 April. The main resistance to the German invasion took place in this village in southern Jutland. During the skirmish a small number of Danish troops were killed and the Germans lost this vehicle to the Danes' Madsen 20mm anti-aircraft/anti-tank guns. During the 'peaceful' invasion the Germans lost four light tanks and had twelve armoured cars and scout cars destroyed or damaged. (Author's Collection)

(**Opposite, above**) A long column of German motor vehicles are stopped on one of the roads which ran through the Jutland region. The invasion was not achieved without some cost to the German Army, with twenty soldiers killed or wounded. In the foreground is a Flak 30 20mm anti-aircraft gun, protecting the column from the non-existent Danish aerial threat. This gun, which could also be used in an anti-tank role, was to provide sterling service to the German Army throughout the war. (*Author's Collection*)

(**Opposite, below**) A German supply column moves along a forest road during the invasion of Denmark on 9 April. As the takeover of Denmark was relatively peaceful, the men have removed their steel helmets. They obviously are not expecting any problems during their advance and there were no instances of spontaneous resistance by the Danish people. The speed and smooth organisation of the invasion stopped any thoughts amongst the population to take up arms. (*Norway Archives*)

(**Above**) A motorised German column is seen in a town close to Copenhagen on the morning of 9 April. Although resistance to the German invasion was minimal, the invaders had to be on their guard regardless. As the Germans advanced across Denmark they usually met the same angry indifference from the shocked population. One thing that the invasion did prove to the outside world was that any countries which regarded their declared neutrality as protection were fooling themselves. (*Author's Collection*)

Laden down with full kit, these German soldiers are marching into Copenhagen on 9 April. The takeover of Denmark was regarded as a sideshow to the main campaign in Norway but its rapid conquest gave Hitler another excuse to demonstrate the might of his armed forces. The German dictator's cynical excuse for invading Denmark was the well used one that he was protecting the country from Allied invasion. (Author's Collection)

General Frederik Christian Essemann leaves his headquarters at Viborg after capitulating to the German forces. He was in command of the 'Jutland' Division, which bore the brunt of the German invasion on 9 April. Accompanying him is a German major who has just accepted the 63-year-old general's surrender. (Cody Images)

German vehicles parked up on the cobbled streets of picturesque Copenhagen as the Danish government was busy coming to terms with the invaders. Some Danish units did put up some resistance in several skirmishes, losing twenty-six killed and twenty-three wounded as a result. The German high command had expected to succeed without any serious resistance from the Danes, but had the Danish Army, Navy and Air Forces put up a substantial fight the Germans were prepared and willing to crush them without mercy. (*Author's Collection*)

Danish women in conversation with a group of German soldiers in the centre of Copenhagen on 10 April. In most occupied countries there were people who were willing to be friendly towards the Germans. But fraternising with the enemy was dangerous and men and women who befriended the invaders would usually suffer consequences upon liberation in 1945. (*Cody Images*)

VOIR PAGE SUIVANTE

(**Opposite, above**) Young Danes argue with a German soldier who is directing traffic on the streets of Copenhagen on the first day of the invasion. Many Danes were not just angry with the Germans, they were also embarrassed by the swift conquest of their country. One German officer who had taken part in the invasions of Czechoslovakia, Poland and now Denmark noted the Danes' reactions compared to other nationalities. He said: 'In Prague they spat at us, in Poland they shot at us, but in Denmark they looked at us like we were a circus act!' The soldier arguing with these Danes appears to be a reservist as he is wearing the M16 steel helmet that was no longer in use with the Wehrmacht. (*Author's Collection*)

(**Opposite, below**) In the centre of Copenhagen these German troops have set up a temporary bivouac with their kit on the ground around them. The occupation of Denmark may have been a relatively easy affair but there was a seething anger amongst the population bubbling under the surface. Most of these troops would not enjoy the pleasures of the Danish capital for long as there were other, more important, conquests to be made. (*Author's Collection*)

(**Above**) German soldiers smile for the camera on the train from Frederikshavn to Copenhagen in the first days of the occupation of Denmark, which began with a 'velvet glove' approach by the Germans in the hope that the Danes would become their allies. From April 1940 to 29 August 1943 Denmark was a German protectorate with its own government and even its own small army. From 1943 until 1945 Denmark was treated as just another occupied country, although the population was still treated better than in other German-controlled countries. (*Author's Collection*)

German troops gather around a Wehrmacht field kitchen in the centre of Copenhagen in the aftermath of the invasion. If the Germans expected to be welcomed by the Danish population they were to be disappointed. Hitler decided to leave a compliant government in charge of Denmark and hoped that the country would be a 'model protectorate'. By 1943 the rise in resistance among the Danes led to a more severe occupation, which involved 170,000 troops. The fact that the equivalent of fourteen divisions were involved in keeping the peace in Denmark instead of being at the front line was a moral victory for the Danes. (Author's Collection)

German troops closed one of the main streets in Copenhagen outside Osterport railway station on 9 April. The iron grip imposed on the Danish capital was intended to stop any signs of resistance to the German takeover. Here Danish civilians look on in silence as their capital is 'peacefully' occupied by the German Army. (Author's Collection)

Chapter Four

The German Invasion of Norway

A plan for the German invasion of Scandinavia – 'Studie Nord' – had been drawn up on 26 February 1940. It called for a large naval invasion force that would involve the majority of the Kriegsmarine's ships. The Kriegsmarine had no history of naval landing operations and no specialist ships to transport troops. It would depend on fighting ships to carry troops and these had little room to accommodate personnel other than their crews. Even though only 9,000 troops were involved in the initial landings in Denmark and Norway, a large number of ships and boats would have to be involved.

The German naval invasion force was made up of eleven groups, with Groups 1 to 6 heading for Norway:

- Group 1, earmarked for Narvik, comprised the battleships *Scharnhorst* and *Gneisenau*, with ten destroyers carrying 2,000 troops;
- Group 2, for Trondheim, comprised the cruiser *Admiral Hipper* and four destroyers carrying 1,700 troops;
- Group 3, for Bergen, comprised the cruisers *Köln* and *Konigsberg*, the service ships *Bremse* and *Karl Peters*, and three torpedo boats and five motor torpedo boats carrying 1,900 troops;
- Group 4, for Kristiansand, comprised the cruiser *Karlsruhe*, the service ship *Tsingtau*, three torpedo boats and seven motor torpedo boats carrying 1,100 troops;
- Group 5, for Oslo, comprised the cruisers *Blücher*, *Lützow* and *Emden*, three torpedo boats, two armed whaling boats and eight minesweepers carrying 2,000 troops; and
- Group 6, for Egersund, comprised four minesweepers carrying 150 troops.

The remaining five Groups were scheduled for the invasion of Denmark. The ships of Groups 7 to 11 were made up smaller boats, minesweepers, tugs, picket boats and merchant vessels. One old battleship, the First World War era *Schleswig-Holstein*, was attached to them to provide artillery support for the landing force at Korsor.

- Group 7, to Korsor and Viborg, carried 1,990 troops;
- Group 8, to Copenhagen, carried 1,000 troops;
- Group 9, to Middlefart, carried 400 troops; and
- Groups 10 to Esbjerg and 11 to Tyboron carried no troops.

The German ground forces earmarked for the invasions of Denmark and Norway were two army corps, XXXI for the attack on Denmark and XXI for the invasion of Norway. In total there were nine divisions in the invasion force, made up of the 170th and 198th Divisions for Denmark and the 69th, 163rd, 181st, 196th and 214th Infantry Divisions for the invasion of Norway. Because of the mountainous terrain in Norway there were also two mountain divisions, the 2nd and 3rd. A large number of aircraft were to be sent to Scandinavia under the umbrella of the X Fliegerkorps under the command of Lieutenant General Hans Geissler. Aircraft in the Fliegerkorps included 290 bombers, 100 fighters, 40 Stuka dive-bombers and 70 reconnaissance floatplanes. The Germans were determined not to underestimate the challenges of getting troops to Scandinavia and supplying them. A huge force of 500 Junkers Ju 52/3m transport planes was to be used to land troops and carry paratroops and to keep them supplied during the course of Operation 'Weserubung'.

The occupation of Denmark had gone to plan and the Danish king was now unable to leave Copenhagen had he wanted to. German plans likewise called for the rapid capture of the Norwegian king and his family, which would hopefully result in their country's quick capitulation. One of the first tasks of the troops landing at Oslo was to capture the king but things did not go according to plan. During the landings the Kriegsmarine's *Blücher* was hit by the guns of the coastal fortress at Oscarsborg and sank with 800 troops aboard. This disaster for the Germans caused a short delay in their operation, which allowed the king, Crown Prince Olav and his family to get away from Oslo. The widowed King Haakon was left alone in the royal palace, and the Crown Prince and his wife Princess Martha were at their Asker estate with their three children. Germany offered the king terms at 4.50 in the morning of 9 April but he, along with the Crown Prince, refused them.

The Norwegians did not surrender even after the capture of their main ports. Their morale had been raised by the sinking of the *Blücher*, which delayed the take-over of Oslo. The Norwegian Army commander-in-chief General Laake did not have the attributes of a wartime commander and was replaced on the 10th by Colonel Ruge, who was regarded as the epitome of a fighting officer and who was raised to the rank of general on the same day. General Ruge quickly tried to organise the disparate units of the Norwegian Army into a viable force capable of fighting the invaders. Some Norwegian commanders, including Ruge, were encouraged to continue to resist by an offer of military aid from Britain and France. King Haakon VII also threatened to abdicate if Norway did not choose to fight, bearing in mind the situation his brother Christian X of Denmark had been forced into by events.

This RAF reconnaissance photograph shows naval activity close to Bergen on 9 April. A Norwegian Navy gunboat has intercepted ships which its captain suspected of being involved with the German invasion. On the 9th the armed forces of Norway were still in shock and in the chaos the various units were operating with limited information. Any Norwegian ships that were near any of the Kriegsmarine target ports were soon dealt with by the German Navy. (Author's Collection)

In a photograph taken just before the campaign, a flotilla of Kriegsmarine destroyers are pictured in the North Sea. The number of destroyers in the German fleet was dwarfed by the number on the strength of the Royal Navy. There were sixty destroyers and smaller warships in the Kriegsmarine, while the Royal Navy had 184 destroyers as well as forty-five escort ships. The losses sustained by the Germans in Norway in 1940 were impossible to replace during the remainder of the war. (*Author's Collection*)

A line of Kriegsmarine destroyers move along the Norwegian coast as they head for their target ports to unload their human cargoes. The German Navy did not have a history of transporting military units by sea and there was a shortage of suitable supply ships. This meant that combat ships had to be utilised to take troops to Norway, which limited the numbers of soldiers who could be landed ashore. (*Author's Collection*)

Kriegsmarine destroyers pictured en-route to Norway in the first days of April, having spent the autumn and winter of 1939/1940 battling the superior Royal Navy. They had four Type 1934s and twelve Type 1934As, as well as six Type 1936s, eight Type 1936As ('Narvik' class), seven Type 1936As ('Mob' class), four Type 1936Bs and two Type 1936Cs. The main advantage that the Germans had over the Royal Navy was the fact that all their destroyers and most of their capital ships were built after 1933. (*Author's Collection*)

(**Above**) German troops sit patiently on an airfield waiting to board the Junkers Ju 52/3m transports behind them. The large fleet of these planes was to prove crucial to the German war machine during the Blitzkrieg era from September 1939 until June 1941. Although the Ju 52 was a relatively old design, having been first produced in 1930, it remained in service until 1945. At the start of the Second World War the Luftwaffe had 533 already in service, with a further 500 being built in 1939–1940. The vast majority of these planes were allocated to the Norwegian Campaign, where they were used in a number of supply roles, as well as for transporting troops and dropping paratroopers. (*Author's Collection*)

(**Opposite, above left**) German troops jump down from the cargo door of a Junkers Ju 52/3m transport plane, the workhorse of the Luftwaffe's aerial supply effort. The 500 Junkers involved in the invasion of Denmark and Norway in April 1940 were soon transferred to other fronts. A total of 4,580 Junkers 52s were built and the affectionately named 'Tante Ju' or 'Aunty Junkers' served until 1945. (*Author's Collection*)

(**Opposite, above right**) A Zundapp motorcycle is manhandled from the cargo door of a Junkers 52/3m as part of the transport effort to supply the German forces in Norway. The Junkers was a slow aircraft with a maximum speed of 178mph, and it was shot down in large numbers when there was serious enemy aerial opposition. They could carry about 10,000lb of cargo or eighteen troops and their kit, and were used during the Norwegian campaign in a wide variety of roles. (*Author's Collection*)

(**Opposite, below**) German troops and sailors unload their kit and supplies at the southern Norwegian port of Kristiansand. Realising that they could not capture all of the fifteen main ports along the long Norwegian coastline, the Germans had to choose a small number of the more strategic ports to attack, including Kristiansand and Oslo in the south. Other southern ports chosen were Bergen and Stavanger, along with Trondheim on the coast of central Norway. By far the most important port to be taken was Narvik, which was, after all, the main reason why the campaign was being fought. (*Author's Collection*)

A lookout stands on the rocky hills around the port of Kristiansand in the first days of its occupation, watching for any signs of Allied activity. The port, which was on the southern coast of Norway, was the target for some of the smaller German ships, which left the main fleet during its journey north. Kristiansand was the site of a major Norwegian Navy base and was stoutly defended by its shore batteries. The batteries prevented the German ships from landing the troops aboard them and even the guns of the cruiser *Karlsruhe* could not silence them. But after several heavy bombing raids on the Norwegian forts by the Luftwaffe, the port fell without further resistance. (*Author's Collection*)

The Kriegsmarine K-class scouting cruiser *Konigsberg* pictured before the Norwegian Campaign. During the landings at Bergen this ship was used to threaten the Norwegian shore batteries at Kharven and Sandviken. Shells from the 21cm guns of the battery at Kharven hit the *Konigsberg* three times, leading to flooding and fire aboard the ship. This forced the cruiser to drop anchor, with its guns still returning fire, until Luftwaffe bombers arrived to silence the battery. *(Author's Collection)*

Kriegsmarine torpedo boats are seen at sea after leaving the port of Bergen during the Norwegian Campaign. The most modern type of torpedo boat in service in Norway was the Type 24, with the Type 35 and Type 39 not entering service until later in the war. During the 1940 campaign the majority of torpedo boats were of First World War vintage, which had the prefix 'T' followed by a three figure number. In the Kriegsmarine torpedo boats were not patrol boats, with the larger ones being slightly smaller than destroyers. *(Author's Collection)*

The German cruisers *Köln*, *Konigsberg* and the aged *Bremse*, escorted by a flotilla of E-boats and two torpedo boats headed for Bergen. Transported aboard the warships and a depot ship were 900 troops tasked with capturing the port. This photograph features *Köln*, with her nine 5.9-inch main guns in three triple gun turrets. Unlike most of the German capital ships, *Köln* was built in the last years of the Weimar Republic rather than during the 1933–1939 Nazi period. (*Author's Collection*)

German troops transfer from the cruisers that had transported them from their home ports to Bergen with 600 troops aboard each ship. From these rubber dinghies they were put aboard smaller boats – torpedo boats, E-boats and launches – and were taken to various points along the coast around Bergen to attack the Norwegian strong-points. During the transfers from cruisers to smaller boats the German troops were vulnerable to Norwegian attacks but an aerial attack by two floatplanes of the Norwegian Naval Air Service caused no real damage. (*Author's Collection*)

Captain Heinrich Woldag of the heavy cruiser *Blücher* and two of his officers pose for the camera shortly before his ship sailed to Norway. On 9 April *Blücher* had dropped off 150 troops to two escorting destroyers when she came under fire from a Norwegian shore battery. Hit by two torpedoes from Oskarborg Fortress, *Blücher* capsized and sank at 07.27am with heavy loss of life. The 970 men who did manage to scramble ashore included both Captain Woldag and Konteradmiral Kummetz.
(Author's Collection)

The Kriegsmarine heavy cruiser *Blücher* pictured days before the invasion of Norway in April. As with other large ships of the German Navy, *Blücher* was tasked with transporting troops to Norway. The second of five Hipper class heavy cruisers, *Blücher* was built in Kiel and launched in 1937. She led the Kriegsmarine force into Oslofjord on the night of 8/9 April and came under attack from the obsolete 11-inch guns of the Norwegian Oscarsborg Fortress. It was, however, the torpedo battery in the fortress that did the damage to the German ship and sealed its fate.
(Author's Collection)

At the end *Blücher* keeled over, the two torpedoes having caused a major fire onboard. This fire spread to the magazine holding anti-aircraft ammunition and then to the fuel bunkers, which caused the ship to quickly capsize and sink to the bottom of the fjord. Lost with the ship were a thousand of the crew, as well as Vice Admiral Kummetz and General Engelbrecht, commander of the 169th Infantry Division. *(Author's Collection)*

A Panzerkampfwagen II Type C light tank after being unloaded from its transport ship in Oslo harbour. It belongs to the 3rd Company of Panzer-Abteilung Zbv 40, whose tanks were designated to play a major role in the takeover of southern Norway. En-route to Norway the transport ship *Antaris H* carrying fifteen tanks was sunk, taking the tanks and their crews down with her. Only this Panzer II and a single Panzer I survived to take part in the invasion. They were reinforced by the 1st and 2nd Companies, which were transferred from Denmark to Norway by 24 April. The 20mm main armament of the Panzer II was a useful weapon against any opposition. *(Author's Collection)*

German troops disembarking from their transport ship in Oslo harbour to be carried to shore aboard a tender. Their landing is protected from interference by the looming presence of the heavy cruiser *Admiral Hipper* on the far side of the harbour. Laid down in 1935, the *Hipper* was launched in February 1937 and entered service with the Kriegsmarine in September 1939. It was one of the few German capital ships which survived until the end of the war, having been kept in port since Hitler ordered the Navy's surface ships to stay in port. He made this decision after the Kriegsmarine's failure to tackle the Allied navies to his satisfaction. (*Author's Collection*)

(**Above**) Newly arrived German troops prepare to move from the harbour into the centre of Oslo on the back of a commandeered civilian truck. These troops were transported to Oslo by the Kriegsmarine's Marine Gruppe 5, which sailed from the German port of Swinemunde. The German invasion was achieved with minimal forces who used a mix of bluff and show of force to take the Norwegian capital. The infantry would drive into Oslo and set up machine guns at strategic points before the Norwegians had time to react. (*National Library of Norway*)

(**Opposite, above**) German troops seen just after disembarking from the Kriegsmarine destroyer in the background. These soldiers would be transported to the centre of the city to take up positions at strategic points. It was hoped that the invasions of Denmark and Norway would be bloodless *coup d'etats*, but in Norway many people were not willing to give in meekly to the pressure exerted by the German armed forces. (*Author's Collection*)

(**Opposite, below**) A German MG34 machine gunner scans the skies above the docks in Oslo on 9 April for any sign of a British-French reaction to the takeover of Norway. The sheer audacity of the German invasion was grudgingly admired by many who did not sympathise with their objectives. For several years the Germans had pushed their luck when it came to their takeovers of Austria and Czechoslovakia and their invasion of Poland. Hitler's later gambles were not to be so successful but in April 1940 he was on the verge of taking over much of Europe. (*Author's Collection*)

(**Opposite, above**) A German military band plays joyful tunes on 9 April as the bemused citizens of Oslo look on. The German plan to sow confusion amongst the population was a great success, aided by Norwegian traitors. With a mix of demonstrations of brute force and signs of normal life going on regardless of the invasion, the Germans were able to subdue the civilians in the Norwegian capital. These men had been flown into Norway aboard a Junkers Ju 52/3m transport plane in the early hours of the invasion. (*Author's Collection*)

(**Opposite, below**) A soldier hands out Mauser 98k rifles to his comrades from the back of a commandeered truck on an Oslo street. The only advantage for the Norwegian and Danish populations was that they were regarded by the Nazis as fellow Aryans. For the Jewish populations, of course, there was more to fear from the German invasion but in the early years all people were treated reasonably well by the occupiers. (*Author's Collection*)

(**Above**) German troops man an MG34 machine gun overlooking the main square in Oslo in the days following the occupation. Whenever the German Army occupied a city or town during the Second World War they established a strong presence on the streets. The obvious intention was to let the civilian population know in no uncertain terms that any resistance would be met with full force. (*Cody Images*)

Two German soldiers stand at the base of the tower of Radio Oslo's transmitting tower on 10 April. Not surprisingly, strategic targets like this were earmarked by the German command for immediate capture when the Germans reached the Norwegian capital. If the invaders had any doubts as to exactly which buildings and strategic points should be captured, the Norwegian 'fifth columnists' were happy to point them out to them. (*Author's Collection*)

(**Opposite, above**) In a show of force a German medium field gun is pulled through the streets of Oslo on the way north to begin the process of consolidating control of Norway. The FH-18 105mm gun was the mainstay of the Wehrmacht's artillery for the rest of the war. Although the Germans made much of their mechanised units during the Blitzkrieg era, most artillery units still relied on horses to transport their guns. (*Norwegian Archives*)

(**Opposite, below**) A long column of German troops marching through the centre of Oslo on 9 April 1940 with a curious and silently hostile crowd looking on. They are marching down the main thoroughfare in Oslo, the Karl Johans Gate, their first day of occupation. It is claimed that the young man holding his bicycle on the left of the photograph is 22-year-old Gunnar Sonsteby, who went on to be a renowned resistance fighter from 1941 until 1945 and was the most highly decorated member of the Norwegian Resistance Movement ('Motstandsbevegelsen'). (*Author's Collection*)

(**Above**) German soldiers man a Maxim M1908 heavy machine gun overlooking Oslo harbour during the Norwegian Campaign. Although the Germany Army had been issued with modern weaponry since 1933, they still had to use some weapons of First World War vintage. Once a country had been occupied, the Germans garrisoned it according to the kind of resistance they expected to face. Hitler hoped that the Scandinavian countries would accept their occupation as he regarded their populations as racially acceptable. (*Author's Collection*)

(**Opposite, above**) This photograph of German troops in the centre of the Norwegian capital was taken on the morning of 11 April. By this time it appeared that the invasion had been a complete success and the population appeared to have accepted the situation. However, some Norwegian units were still opposing the Germans and waiting hopefully for assistance from the British and French. (*Norwegian Archives*)

(**Opposite, below**) Behind two Junkers Ju 52/3m transport planes on the runway of Oslo airport burns the wreck of an RAF bomber. Raids by the RAF over Norway during the campaign were usually performed at night by a mixed force of bombers. At this stage in the war any bomber that reached Norway would have only a limited time over the target before having to return to their British bases. (*Author's Collection*)

The German destroyer Z16 *Friedrich Eckoldt* at anchor off Trondheim where she landed a number of troops on 9 April. She had transported soldiers of the 138th Gebirgsjager Regiment, who helped seize the port. All the ships that had taken part in the Norway landings were short of fuel but vital oil was transferred from another destroyer to Z16. On the 12th, after more oil was found, the Z16 set sail for Germany and took no further part in the Norwegian Campaign. (*Author's Collection*)

Newly arrived German troops stand around on a street corner in Trondheim, the second most important city in Norway after the capital. The first assault troops had landed at Trondheim at 4.25am on 9 April and immediately fanned out to capture all the important buildings. There was no resistance from the Norwegian troops stationed at the port and its magnificent harbour was soon full of Kriegsmarine ships. (*Author's Collection*)

Trondheim airfield in the early days of the Norwegian Campaign, full of Junkers Ju 52/3m transports. In most of the cities captured by the Germans in early April there was a need to reinforce their garrisons quickly. At the height of the campaign in April and May the Luftwaffe's 500-strong force of Ju 52s played a pivotal role in the German victory. Moving supplies and reinforcements from town to town by road was difficult when parts of Norway were in Allied hands. These aircraft allowed the German Army to expand the territory under their control, knowing that ammunition and other supplies could be quickly dispatched when needed by plane. (*Author's Collection*)

Gebirgsjagers are being fitted with life-jackets by a member of the ship's crew taking them to Narvik. They are part of the 1,900 mountain troops from the 139th Mountain Regiment of the 3rd Mountain Division. Under the command of General Dietl, these men were to form the backbone of the garrison of the vital port of Narvik. (*Author's Collection*)

The Norwegian coastal defence ship *Eidsvold* in pre-war days at anchor in Oslo harbour. This ship, launched in 1899, was the oldest ironclad still in service in 1940 and was totally outdated. A Norwegian admiral affectionately called *Eidsvold* and her sister ship *Norge*, launched in 1900, 'my old bathtubs'. In the days before the war the two ironclads were sent to defend the vital port of Narvik in the north, but when they tried to challenge the Kriegsmarine vessels approaching Narvik they were blown to bits. (*Author's Collection*)

Captain Odd Isaachsen Willoch, commander of the Norwegian coastal defence ship HNoMS *Eidsvold*. On 9 April his obsolete and under-gunned ship faced a superior Kriegsmarine force as he tried to defend the port of Narvik. Although he was facing ten German destroyers, Willoch refused to surrender and radioed to his superiors that he was 'ready to attack'. A German officer came aboard *Eidsvold* to try to persuade the Norwegian captain to give up the hopeless fight but after he had left the heroic Willoch issued an instruction to his crew, saying 'Man the guns. We're going to fight, boys!' Within minutes *Eidsvold* was hit by three German torpedoes and blew up, breaking in two and sinking in just fifteen seconds. Only six of the doomed ship's crew survived the one-sided battle and the captain was not amongst them. (*Author's Collection*)

HMS *Rodney* was one of the most powerful battleships in the Royal Navy in early 1940, with a displacement of 33,900 tons and nine 16-inch main guns as well as twelve 6-inch guns and six 4.7-inch anti-aircraft guns. On 9 April *Rodney* was part of a naval task force whose objective was to try to hamper the German invasion of Norway. During the operation while sailing off Karmey she was hit by a bomb from a Luftwaffe bomber which penetrated the ship's armoured deck but failed to explode. Despite the damage she suffered, *Rodney* continued to serve in Norwegian waters until the end of the land campaign. (*Author's Collection*)

(**Above**) On 9 April the light cruiser HMS *Southampton* was in Norwegian waters when she was attacked by Luftwaffe planes. During the attack the ship suffered shell damage and her control system for the main battery was knocked out. Although the damage was temporarily repaired by the crew, the ship was called back to home waters for further repairs. However, instead of then returning to Norway the ship was kept in England as part of the anti-invasion naval force stationed along the south coast. In this photograph *Southampton* is seen moving along the Norwegian coastline in the days before the beginning of the fighting. (*Author's Collection*)

(**Opposite, above**) On the evening of 9 April it was decided to send a message to the Germans that their invasion of Scandinavia would not go unchallenged. An RAF bomber force was put together, made up of twelve Armstrong Whitworth Whitley Mk IV and twelve Handley Page Hampden medium bombers. Their raid on the German forces which had landed at the Norwegian port of Bergen the same day was not particularly successful. No substantial targets were hit during the attack, although the press reported 'near misses' on several German ships. One plane was lost but the long distances and poor weather that the bomber crews had to deal with could have resulted in much higher losses. Here the crew of one of the Hampdens pose for the press after their arduous journey to Norway and back. (*Author's Collection*)

(**Left**) The crew of HMS *Spearfish*, an S-class submarine, show off their ship's motif painted on the conning tower. They are being congratulated for their success in damaging the German heavy cruiser *Lützow* on 11 April. She had been patrolling in the Kattegat, an area of sea bordered by southern Norway, northern Denmark and south-west Sweden. Although their torpedo did not sink *Lützow*, the German ship was out of action for a year at a crucial period of the sea war with Britain.
(*Author's Collection*)

The Kriegsmarine heavy cruiser *Lützow* moored in harbour before the Norwegian Campaign. She was launched in 1931 under her original name *Deutschland*, but her name was changed in early 1940, reportedly to avoid the possibility of a ship named after the Fatherland being sunk. When she was hit by a torpedo from the Royal Navy submarine HMS *Spearfish* the damage was sufficient to take a year to repair. She had previously been damaged during the Battle of Drobak in Oslofjord on 9 April during which the *Blücher* had been sunk. It was decided to return immediately to Germany for repairs and it was during her journey home that HMS *Spearfish* struck. (*Author's Collection*)

Chapter Five

The Narvik Sea Battles, 10–13 April

In the aftermath of the German landings in Denmark and Norway on 9 April the Franco-British Allies had to react in some way. While they began to prepare to bring their own ground forces to Norway, they needed to answer German aggression in some way. It was most feasible for the Royal Navy to attack the Germans at sea rather than try to counter them by air or on land. Anchored in Narvik harbour in the north of Norway were a number of German transport ships and a strong force of Kriegsmarine destroyers. The warships and transports had only just finished unloading when a Royal Navy force appeared. On the morning of 10 April Captain B.A.W. Warburton-Lee led his 2nd Flotilla into Ofotfjord. His five H-class destroyers – HMS *Hotspur*, HMS *Hostile*, HMS *Hardy*, HMS *Hunter* and HMS *Havoc* – gathered intelligence as they moved up the Norwegian coast. Warburton-Lee was informed by Norwegian sources that the German force anchored at Narvik was made up of six German destroyers under the command of Kommodore Friedrich Bonte. He also learned that the Kriegsmarine ships were armed, crucially, with 5-inch guns while his own ships had 4.7-inch main armament. This apparently minor difference in calibre was important as it gave the German ships more hitting power and they could fire a shell twice the size of the British shells. Warburton's Norwegian informers advised him that he would need far more ships if he wanted to take on the German force, but Warburton-Lee was a brave and honourable commander who was not going to be deterred from obeying his orders by this bad news. The German fleet which the Royal Navy force was to encounter was in fact made up of ten destroyers, Z-2 *Georg Thiele*, Z-9 *Wolfgang Zenker*, Z-11 *Bernd von Arnim*, Z-12 *Erich Giese*, Z-13 *Erich Koellner*, Z-17 *Diether von Roeder*, Z-18 *Hans Ludermann*, Z-19 *Hermann Kunne*, Z-21 *Anton Schmitt* and Z-22 *Wilhelm Heidkamp*. When Warburton-Lee's 2nd Flotilla arrived at Narvik at 4.30am they entered the harbour and quickly sank two German destroyers, Z-21 and Z-22. They also damaged the Z-17 in what became a brutal close-quarter shoot-out with the Kriegsmarine ships. When the Royal Navy ships were engaged by ground troops in Narvik they decided to leave the harbour, and were then ambushed by three German destroyers, Z-9, Z-13 and Z-12, which sallied out of the Herjangfjord. This force was then joined by another two destroyers, Z-2 and Z-11, which came out of Ballangen Bay. In the ensuing battle HMS *Hardy* ended up beaching in flames with a mortally wounded Warburton-Lee on board. HMS *Hunter* was torpedoed and sunk by the German destroyers while HMS *Hotspur* was badly damaged. The surviving British ships now left the scene, while a blocking force led by the cruiser HMS *Penelope* made sure that the German ships did not leave the port.

A few days after the first battle at Narvik a stronger Royal Navy force was assembled to go back to the port to finish off the surviving Kriegsmarine destroyers. This force, under the command of Vice Admiral Whitworth, was headed by the battleship HMS *Warspite* supported by nine destroyers, four of them from the Tribal class: HMS *Bedouin*, HMS *Cossack*, HMS *Punjabi* and HMS *Eskimo*. The other five destroyers were HMS *Kimberley*, HMS *Hero*, HMS *Icarus*, HMS *Forester* and HMS *Foxhound*. Also assigned to the force was the aircraft-carrier HMS *Furious*, with Fairy Swordfish torpedo-bombers aboard. When the leading destroyers moved into Ofotfjord on the morning of 13 April they found the eight remaining Kriegsmarine destroyers now under the command of Frigate Captain Erich Bey. The German ships lacked fuel and ammunition and were not really prepared for the coming battle. Even before the main battle began a Swordfish from *Furious* found and sank the only German submarine in the area, *U64*. When the serious fighting started it was a one-sided and brutal affair, with three German destroyers being swiftly sunk. The guns of HMS *Warspite* made short work of these ships, with Z-13 the first to be sunk, followed shortly by the Z-19. Four German destroyers, Z-2, Z-9, Z-11 and Z-18, retreated to the far end of the fjord, where their crews scuttled them. On the Royal Navy side HMS *Bedouin* was slightly damaged, while HMS *Eskimo* lost her bows to German fire. HMS *Punjabi* and HMS *Cossack* were also damaged by fire from the German destroyers before they were in turn put out of action. This second battle of Narvik cost the Kriegsmarine dearly – 1,000 dead and 50 per cent of their destroyers either sunk or put out of action. Some 2,600 survivors from the destroyers' crews now became ground troops as part of the Narvik garrison. Although the Royal Navy also lost a number of ships during the two battles, they were able to withstand these losses better than the Germans could.

HMS *Hunter*, an H-class destroyer, took part in the first battle of Narvik on 10 April. Her main armament was four 4.7-inch guns and her anti-aircraft protection came from two quadruple 0.5-inch machine guns. On 6 April *Hunter* protected the minelayers laying a minefield in the vicinity of Narvik. Four days later she joined the Royal Navy destroyer force which attacked the Kriegsmarine ships in Narvik harbour. After this first action *Hunter* led the other destroyers out of Narvik, where they were met by five more German destroyers. In the confusion *Hunter* was accidentally rammed by HMS *Hotspur*, and then was shelled by the German destroyers. She capsized and 107 of her crew were lost, with another five dying of their wounds. Forty-six others were rescued by enemy ships. (*Author's Collection*)

One of the Kriegsmarine destroyers in the vicinity of Narvik before the Royal Navy attack. These ships had carried a large part of the German land forces involved in the invasion of Norway. The German Navy had been quickly expanded after Adolf Hitler's rise to power but there was no way it could rival the sheer number of vessels in the Royal Navy. (*Author's Collection*)

The confused situation in Narvik harbour after the first battle of Narvik on 10 April is apparent in this photograph. There was little time for the Germans to prepare for any further attacks but they did what they could to be ready for the expected second wave of Royal Navy ships. During the first battle both the British commander Captain B.A.W. Warburton-Lee and his German counterpart Kommodore Friedrich Bonte lost their lives. *(Author's Collection)*

In the aftermath of the first battle of Narvik a German merchant ship burns in the harbour. During both the battles at Narvik a large number of powerful German and Royal Navy ships were crammed into a relatively compact area to fight it out. This close-quarter fighting resulted in the loss of many of the ships participating in the battle and many merchant vessels in the harbour. *(Author's Collection)*

This photograph shows Narvik harbour in the few days between the first battle of Narvik on 10 April and the second battle on the 13th. The harbour is strewn with the wrecks of Kriegsmarine and German merchant ships sunk in the first battle. German commanders prepared as best they could for a second attack on the port and one destroyer, Z-13 *Erich Koeller*, which had run aground, was set up as a floating battery. Another ship, Z-17 *Diether von Roeder*, which had been damaged, was crewed to act as harbour defence. (*Author's Collection*)

HMS *Icarus* was an I-class destroyer built in the mid-1930s. She saw action in the seas around Norway in April 1940. Her first action was the capture of the 8,514-ton German transport ship *Alster*, which she took on 11 April. Having escorted *Alster* back to the UK to be crewed by merchant marine sailors under her new name *Empire Endurance*, *Icarus* returned to Norway where she took part in the second battle of Narvik, acting as a minesweeper for the Royal Navy battleship HMS *Warspite*. On 23 April *Icarus* was involved in the landings by British troops at the Norwegian port of Åndalsnes. (*Author's Collection*)

The original caption to this photograph describes the task force of Royal Navy destroyers moving up Ofotfjord to attack the Kriegsmarine destroyers sheltering in Narvik harbour. It was taken on the afternoon of 13 April when HMS *Warspite* was leading the destroyers towards their target. According to the caption, the destroyers used minesweeping and other anti-mine practices as they moved along the Norwegian coast. Waiting for them in Narvik harbour were the German destroyers which had survived the first battle on the 10th. (*Author's Collection*)

The pom-pom anti-aircraft guns on a Royal Navy ship fire at an attacking Luftwaffe plane during a battle at sea in April 1940. During the Norwegian Campaign the Royal Navy had a great advantage over the much smaller Kriegsmarine, but this was partly countered by the ever-present Luftwaffe bombers and dive-bombers that dominated the skies. Anti-aircraft gun crews were often fighting for the very survival of their ship and to avoid the terrible fate suffered by sailors who ended up in the seas off Norway. (*Author's Collection*)

(**Opposite, above**) The Royal Navy battleship HMS *Warspite* led the destroyer force sent to avenge the defeat of 10 April. With the task force's commander, Vice Admiral William Whitworth, aboard, *Warspite* acted as his flagship. Destroyers attached to the force included four Tribal-class destroyers, HMS *Bedouin*, *Cossack*, *Punjabi* and *Eskimo*. There were also five other destroyers, HMS *Kimberley*, *Hero*, *Icarus*, *Forester* and *Foxhound*. In support of the task force were aircraft flying from the aircraft-carrier HMS *Furious*. When this substantial force arrived in Ofotfjord leading to Narvik they were faced by eight surviving Kriegsmarine destroyers. (*Author's Collection*)

(**Opposite, below**) An unidentified Kriegsmarine Type 1934 destroyer photographed off the Norwegian coast during the sea battles near Narvik. This ship is most likely Z-2 *Georg Thiele*, which was the only destroyer of this class to see service in Norway in 1940. She was severely damaged during the second battle of Narvik and was scuttled by her crew in its aftermath. (*Author's Collection*)

(**Above**) The German destroyer Z-22 *Wilhelm Heidkamp* was one of those that took part in the second battle of Narvik and served as Kommodore Friedrich Bonte's flagship. She was hit in her aft magazine at 5.30am by salvoes from HMS *Hardy* and blew up. Eighty-one sailors were killed, and amongst the dead was the German commander. He was posthumously awarded the Knights Cross in October 1940 on the orders of Adolf Hitler. (*Author's Collection*)

(**Below**) Photographed from a Royal Navy destroyer, three bombs from a Luftwaffe bomber land in the sea astern of the ship. In the close-quarter exchanges between the opposing destroyer flotillas at Narvik most ships suffered damage on 13 April. In addition to the ship to ship bombardments, the activities of the Luftwaffe and the planes of the Fleet Air Arm also caused losses on both sides. (*Author's Collection*)

This out-of-focus image shows the jubilant young gun crews of the Royal Navy Tribal-class destroyer HMS *Punjabi* after the second battle of Narvik. Their relief at surviving the battle is palpable. They are standing in front of their 4.7-inch gun; *Punjabi* had four of these guns, as well as three multi-barrelled anti-aircraft guns. (*Author's Collection*)

This gunnery control telephone operator was photographed on the bridge of one of the Royal Navy destroyers off Narvik. It was the expertise of sailors like this that ensured the success of the destroyer flotilla in their sea battle with Kriegsmarine destroyers. The second battle of Narvik on 13 April saw seven German destroyers sunk and was a major blow for the much smaller Kriegsmarine. (*Author's Collection*)

HMS *Punjabi* at anchor in Skelfjord, having suffered damage during the second battle of Narvik on 13 April. During the battle she had acted as a screening ship for the main destroyer force fighting the Kriegsmarine. Having taken on a number of German destroyers, *Punjabi* had eventually limped into the safety of the fjord. After temporary repairs the ship returned to Devonport dockyard where more thorough repairs were made. (*Author's Collection*)

This Kriegsmarine destroyer was disabled during the fighting on 13 April and subsequently abandoned by its crew. It was one of seven ships sunk during the battle and she drifted for hours before finally sinking. At one time she was reported to be aflame from stem to stern while in Narvik harbour. (Author's Collection)

A German destroyer on fire in the aftermath of the second battle of Narvik, during which all the Kriegsmarine ships were either sunk or put out of action. This photograph was 'doctored' by the Nazi propaganda machine, with a German bomber added to the sky above the ship. The intention was that the German public would believe that the burning vessel was a Royal Navy ship that had been hit by this 'phantom' bomber.
(Author's Collection)

Damage done to an unnamed Royal Navy destroyer, pictured in the aftermath of the second battle of Narvik. According to the original caption, the ship's pinnace (or lifeboat) was destroyed by a German shell. In addition, her funnel took several hits during the fierce sea battle fought off the Norwegian coast. *(Author's Collection)*

Chapter Six

The Germans Advance

Although the German invasions of Denmark and Norway had gone more or less to plan the situation was still in the balance. In the immediate aftermath of the invasion of Norway on 9 April the Germans were in tentative control of a number of ports. They had selected the most strategic ports to take control of: Stavanger, Trondheim, Kristiansand, Bergen, Narvik and the capital Oslo. The disaster suffered by the Kriegsmarine in the sea battles at Narvik on 10 and 13 April left these ports isolated, and the Luftwaffe was tasked to supply them until more troops could arrive to consolidate the German hold on Norway. It was obvious that an Allied Expeditionary force was on its way and over the next few weeks the available troops in the south would have to expand their hold in southern, eastern and central Norway. From the available forces in Oslo a number of small columns were organised to advance northwards to reinforce the port of Trondheim. Small columns also moved north-westwards from Oslo to take towns along the Numedal and Hallingdal valleys.

Two larger columns were also organised. A battle group was created under the command of Lieutenant General Richard Pellengahr (Kampfgruppe Pellengahr). Comprising two infantry battalions, a mechanised machine gun regiment and supporting artillery, it totalled some 4,000 men. Its units were the 196 Infantry Division (340, 345, 362 Regiments), plus 223 Artillery Regiment, 223 Aufklarungs Abt, and 223 Panzerabwehr Abt with one heavy tank and six light tanks. This force was to advance up the Gudbrandsdal valley, with the town of Lillehammer as one of its main objectives. After taking this town it was to continue in a north-westerly direction, by-passing a number of towns before eventually taking Dombås before advancing on the port of Åndalsnes. Dombås had been captured on 14 April by a small force of German paratroops but they were soon overwhelmed by a strong Norwegian unit.

A second, smaller, Kampfgruppe was raised under the command of Oberst Hermann Fischer with a few light tanks. Its objectives were to advance northwards up the Østerdal valley, take the town of Elverum and move past Stor lake.

Facing the Germans advancing through Norway in mid-April were the remains of the Norwegian Army along with a few Fokker CVE light bombers. The six divisions of the Norwegian Army had been stationed all over Norway when the invasion began on 9 April. The 1st Division under the command of General Erichson was in the south-east of the country. He managed to raise 4,000 men who fought for a week before being pushed over the border into Sweden. The 2nd Division, located to the north-west of the 1st, was under the command of General Huinden Haug. King Haakon and his son, Crown Prince Olav, were under the protection of the 2nd, whose units had to withdraw under pressure from German forces. Little was known about the situation with the 3rd Division, which was stationed to the north of the port of Namsos, with 3,000 men. General Steffans had managed to organise units of the 4th Division into a brigade-strong force. Operating around the port of Trondheim was the 5th Division, with its main unit being the 5th Brigade. This brigade, at half its usual strength, was under the command of Colonel Getz and each soldier had about 100 bullets each. Getz's force included a heavy machine gun squadron of dismounted dragoons. In the far north of Norway was the 6th Division, under the command of General Fliescher, whose unit was cut off from the rest of the country by the rugged terrain. He had the strongest division in the Norwegian Army and acted for most of the campaign independently of the other formations, with his unit gaining the epitaph the 'Forgotten Army'.

In addition to the main advance of the German Army through southern and central Norway, there were also other operations taking place to consolidate their hold on the country. A German force was dispatched to try to establish better communication and links between Oslo and the port of Bergen. This advance was countered by light resistance from the Norwegians until the Germans reached the mountain town of Bagn on 18 April. Held by the Norwegian 4th Brigade, the town was being attacked by a pincer movement supported by light tanks. From the hills around the town the Norwegians attacked the Germans, who were largely restricted to the roads through valleys. The Norwegian resistance lasted for two days, with their troops hitting the German tanks from the surrounding hills. The resistance was so strong that the Germans were forced to withdraw back to their base at Hønefoss to the north-west of Oslo. But renewed German attacks and constant bombing raids began to undermine the Norwegian resistance. On 1 May the 300 officers and 3,200 Norwegian soldiers of the 4th Brigade surrendered, giving the Germans complete control of the Oslo-Bergen road. In eight days the Germans had advanced 130 miles from Oslo to Rena, which was General Ruge's first headquarters, and 120 miles from the capital to Lillehammer, his second headquarters.

(**Opposite, above**) The loss of fifteen German tanks during the invasion was a major blow for the German forces, who were left with a Panzer I and a Panzer II until reinforcements could arrive from Denmark. On 19 April three large experimental tanks (designated Neubaufahrzeug Nb Fz) belonging to the Pz Abt.z.b. V.40 'Special Purpose' Unit arrived in Norway. All three are seen here in the centre of Oslo. They were intended by their sheer size to overawe the Norwegian population and were not expected to see much front-line action. However, all three were used during the campaign, but they either broke down or were put out of action by enemy fire. There was no intention for them to be used again in action and the tanks were reported to have been scrapped in 1941. (*Author's Collection*)

(**Below**) Norwegian youths gather curiously around one of the large Neubaufahrzeug Nb Fz tanks that were brought to Oslo in April 1940. This heavy tank is one of five prototypes designed in the first years of Adolf Hitler's rule. The original tanks were called 'Grosstraktors' as a cover name for their military role and were tested secretly in the Soviet Union. At first it was intended to be a multi-turreted tank similar to those being produced in France, Britain and the USSR. The three tanks that were sent to Norway had a main turret with a 75mm Kwk L/24 main armament and a smaller turret at the front armed with machine guns. These leviathans were principally intended to impress the population of Norway by their sheer size but all three saw action during the campaign. (*Library of Congress*)

(**Above**) The next four photographs show German troops being transported along the main railway line running north from Oslo to the port of Bergen. German troops were trained to take advantage of any available transport and the railways were obviously going to be utilised by them. In the early advances through Norway the Germans were not sure how much opposition they would face from the Norwegian Army. At the centre of this group the commanding officer keeps a keen look out for any Norwegian Army units still resisting. During the German advance it was not so much force of arms that proved important but the speed and forcefulness of their attacks that won many actions. (*Author's Collection*)

(**Opposite, above**) In this close-up of the same group featured in the previous photograph the German troops are looking upwards to check for enemy snipers in the rocks above the railway. Having captured the main cities and ports of Norway, the Germans enjoyed a short break before beginning to advance into the rest of the country. During the first days and weeks of the campaign the only opposition to these advances came from Norwegians willing to fight the invaders. (*Author's Collection*)

(**Opposite, below**) Heavily armed German soldiers manning the rear truck of an advancing train. As well as their own MG34 light machine gun, these troops have also acquired a Norwegian heavy machine gun. The only advantage for the Norwegians trying to counter these German advances was their familiarity with the terrain in which they were fighting. (*Author's Collection*)

Troops scramble down from the goods wagon carrying them along a railway going north from Oslo through southern Norway to deal with enemy fire. Any Norwegian resistance was met the customary brute force. However, the Germans did not regard the Norwegians fighting them as guerrillas, and prisoners were taken with a degree of civilisation not seen in Poland in 1939 or from 1941 in Russia and the Balkans. (*Author's Collection*)

A German heavy artillery gun is moved out of the northern suburbs of Oslo on the way to fight in the north, with the crew huddled together on the gun's limber to keep warm. This 105mm leichte Feldhaubitze 18 field gun belongs to AR 233 of the 196th Infantry Division under the command of Lieutenant General Pellengahr. *(Author's Collection)*

This German medium field gun brought north from Oslo has reached the town of Gjøvik. The town stands on the western shore of Lake Mjøsa, which narrows before it reaches the strategic town of Lillehammer. All artillery in the Norwegian Campaign was horse-drawn, as is this 105mm leichte Feldhaubitze 16 which dates back to the First World War. Three of the smiling and relaxed crew smoke pipes as they travel along through the pine forests of southern Norway. *(Author's Collection)*

A unit of Norwegian troops wait in the woods above a town which they are hoping to defend against the German advance through southern Norway. Many Norwegian units were makeshift, with sections, platoons and companies from different units joining together. Infantry, cavalry, artillerymen, redundant pilots and sailors and even members of local ski clubs were recruited into fighting battalions. These included veterans who fought alongside raw recruits and untrained civilian volunteers who were given hasty battle training. (*Author's Collection*)

Two Norwegian soldiers at a mobilisation point where soldiers gathered to be organised into ad hoc units. In the chaos caused by the German capture of the major cities in early April the mobilisation was always going to be difficult. These two young soldiers wear the typical uniforms of the Norwegian Army in 1940, with one wearing the M35 steel helmet and the other an M14 Jager model cap which was introduced as part of the 1914 issue uniform. *(Author's Collection)*

Young Norwegian civilian volunteers are being trucked to a military concentration point where they will be issued with uniforms and weapons. They left their towns and villages to try to reach those Norwegian units that were still fighting in early April. Some joined composite units which were pulled together from remnants of the pre-invasion Norwegian Army. *(Author's Collection)*

Norwegian troops gather around a civilian truck carrying their kit and other supplies as they mobilise in eastern Norway. They would have to counter the eastern column of German troops under the command of General Pellengahr, which was advancing northwards from Oslo. Some of these troops would flee across the Swedish border when they were defeated in mid-April. (*Author's Collection*)

A Norwegian infantry unit is being inspected by its NCO before going out on a patrol as they try to stop the German advance. The advanced age of several of the men indicates the army's reliance on reserves to bolster its numbers. All the troops are wearing the standard M1914 grey-green uniform and have the ski type cap and are armed with Krag-Jorgensen M1894 rifles. The white or grey thick woollen socks are pulled up over the uniform breeches to keep their lower legs warm. (Author's Collection)

The Norwegian commander-in-chief from 10 April, General Otto Ruge is pictured during the early days of the campaign. In the confusing first days of the fighting Ruge managed to create some kind of order from the chaos caused by the German invasion. His efforts were frustrated by poor communication between the dispersed Norwegian units still fighting after the 9th. Continued resistance from the Norwegians in 1940 was largely credited to the Ruge's stoic attitude and his point-blank refusal to surrender to the Germans. (Author's Collection)

Three Norwegian soldiers stand behind an overturned truck which is part of a road-block to halt or at least delay the German advance. They are outside the village of Skanes, which lay to the east of the capital, Oslo. The Norwegian army commander, General Ruge, emphasised to his officers that they should resist for as long as was practical. What he didn't want them to do was waste men and equipment in battles that could not be won. He knew that there would be no reinforcements available, either of manpower or in ammunition and weaponry. *(Author's Collection)*

German troops armed with an MG34 light machine gun take shelter in a ditch while a Panzer I engages Norwegian troops at the village of Haugsbygd. This village to the north-west of Oslo was the scene of one of the early clashes between Norwegian troops and Germans as they advanced into southern and central Norway from the capital. The troops have fitted white snow covers to their M35 helmets but they haven't been issued with snow suits to cover their grey-green uniforms. *(Author's Collection)*

Germany artillerymen manhandle a piece of heavy artillery during the advance from Oslo into central Norway. The Germans had to deal with the country's rugged terrain with few if any motorised vehicles available to pull artillery. In 1940, 105mm guns were used in some numbers by the German Army but larger 150mm guns like the one seen here were few and far between. (*Author's Collection*)

Two German soldiers on the alert during their advance through southern Norway. The man armed with a 1930 EMP sub-machine gun is wearing an M16 steel helmet instead of the standard M35 as worn by his comrade. It appears that small numbers of these First World War era helmets were in use with second-line troops during the Norwegian Campaign. (*Author's Collection*)

(**Above**) German troops move carefully into Bagn valley near the village of Sør-Aurdal during the fighting in southern Norway in mid-April. They are acting as scouts for the mechanised column moving up from the Norwegian capital to expand the territory in German hands. During the early advance through southern and then central Norway the only resistance came from Norwegian units. *(Bagn Bygdesamling)*

(**Opposite, above**) Hauptmann Stemmer stares fiercely at the press photographer documenting the fighting for the town of Bagn. The propaganda newsreels and pictorial magazines back in Germany constantly demanded photographs to show to the public. It was important for the Nazi regime to show its people that their armed forces were achieving great successes. One weakness of the German war machine in Norway is shown by the fact that their armoured force relied largely on light tanks like the Panzer I A in the background. Stemmer's unit was the 40th Panzer Special Battalion, which provided armoured support for the advance in April 1940. *(Author's Collection)*

(**Opposite, below**) A German officer inspects the damage done to a Panzer I light tank during the fighting for the town of Bagn on 18 April. This tank has broken its track and is disabled until a repair crew can get some spares to it. Its crew have removed the two machine guns from its turret, perhaps suggesting that it will not be brought back into action quickly. *(Author's Collection)*

A Ju 87 Stuka ground-attack plane drops its bombs on Norwegian troops during the fighting between them and the German Army at the town of Bagn. The Norwegians were plagued by regular attacks by these deadly planes on any of their units that tried to organise themselves. Such attacks were reported to have a demoralising effect on Norwegian troops during the campaign. (*Author's Collection*)

(**Opposite, above**) In a typical scene from the German advance through southern and central Norway an MG34 machine gun team use the shelter of a Panzer I light tank as they try to establish where enemy fire is coming from. The fighting was basically a series of skirmishes with scratch Norwegian units trying to stop the German columns moving northwards. As the fighting progressed, the German forces in Norway grew stronger while the Norwegian defenders grew ever weaker. (*Author's Collection*)

(**Opposite, below**) This German medium mortar crew is laying down support fire for troops moving along the road to Bagn. The Germans faced heavy resistance from Norwegian troops fighting in the defence of the town. They are firing an 81mm Granatwerfer 34, which was the standard mortar of the German Army throughout the Second World War. (*Author's Collection*)

As the Germans move up towards the town of Bagn, they use a cliff face to provide some cover from Norwegian fire. All the members of this machine gun squad are wearing standard Wehrmacht uniforms in the bitterly cold conditions in Norway. These men have broken away from Kampfgruppe Pellengahr to deal with a large concentration of Norwegian troops at the town. (*Author's Collection*)

A Panzer I light tank moves past a fallen tree which Norwegian troops felled to slow down the German advance. Heavy resistance to the German advance at the mountain town of Bagn went on for two days. The Norwegian 4th Brigade faced superior forces on the ground and constant Stuka and bomber attacks from the air. On 1 May the Norwegians had had enough and the 4th Brigade's remaining 300 officers and 3,200 men surrendered. Norwegian resistance was based around the hope that the Allies would come to their rescue, as promised by the British prime minister, Neville Chamberlain. (*Author's Collection*)

This photograph shows a German unit dealing with a hastily built road-block under the cover of a Panzer I tank. Norwegian troops defending Bagn put up a brave fight and their resistance came as a shock to the over-confident German forces. After defeating the lightly armed Norwegians, the Germans gained new respect for their adversaries. (Author's Collection)

(**Above**) A German paratrooper jumps from a Junkers Ju 52/3m transport plane over Norway as part of the attempt to take the town of Dombås. On 16 April some 200 paratroopers of the 1st Regiment, 7th Flieger Division took the town, which lies mid-way between Lillehammer and Åndalsnes. They faced overwhelming resistance from Allied forces comprising mainly Norwegian units, including the 1st and 2nd Battalions, 11th Regiment, and 1 Company of the 5th Regiment. There was also a machine gun platoon formed from Norwegian Air Force personnel, which had the support of a British 40mm Bofors gun. The German paratroops were forced to surrender on 20 April, having suffered heavy casualties, and 150 of them were taken prisoner after their failed operation. (*Author's Collection*)

(**Opposite, above**) A Panzer I light tank halts at the end of a railway bridge to cover German troops investigating the tunnel on the far side. During the fighting both German and Allied troops used the Norwegian railway system to move from front to front. British troops used the railway tunnels through the mountains of Norway to shelter from Luftwaffe planes on several occasions. (*Author's Collection*)

(**Opposite, below left**) One of the crew of a 20mm Flak 30 anti-aircraft gun uses an optical range-finder to scan the skies for enemy planes during the German advance through central Norway. Before a few RAF planes arrived in mid-April, there was no air real opposition to the Luftwaffe. A few Norwegian light bombers were still being flown but they were used as liaison planes keeping the disparate units in contact with their high command. (*Author's Collection*)

(**Opposite, below right**) After the surrender of a Norwegian unit, one of the soldiers has been given the task of collecting together their rifles. In the early stages of the campaign several Norwegian divisions either surrendered or crossed over the Swedish border. The 1st Division was interned in Sweden, while the 3rd and 4th Divisions surrendered to the Germans in southern Norway. (*Author's Collection*)

Chapter Seven

The Allies Arrive in Norway

The decision to send a military force to Norway was made by the British and French governments soon after the German invasion on 9 April. Both governments felt obliged to support the Norwegian Army that was still resisting the Germans. British Prime Minister Neville Chamberlain had promised King Haakon VII that help would be sent. The expeditionary corps to be sent to Norway was made up of a mix of British and French troops and exiled Poles who had been formed into their own units in the French Army. Landings would have to take place at the smaller ports along the Norwegian coastline as the major ports of Kristiansand, Bergen, Trondheim and Stavanger were in German hands. Narvik's strategic importance to the Allied cause was shown by the arrival of the British 24th Guards Brigade 55 miles to the west of the port on 14 April. This brigade, given the code-name 'Rupert Force', landed at the small port of Harstad, which was already the HQ of the Norwegian 6th Division.

With Allied troops ashore at Narvik, the rest of the North-Western Expeditionary Corps was given the objective of taking the vital port of Trondheim. Two separate forces would be landed to the north and south of the port so that it could be captured by a pincer movement. On 16 April the British 146th Brigade (code-named 'Maurice Force') was landed at the port of Namsos, 119 miles to the north of Trondheim. This force was under the overall command of Major General Adrian Carton de Wiart, with Brigadier Philips as field commander. During the campaign the British were to be reinforced by the French 5th Demi-Brigade, which joined the British in their advance towards Trondheim. On 18 April a second British brigade, the 148th (code-named 'Sickle Force'), under the command of Major General B.T.C. Paget, landed at the port of Åndalsnes, 187 miles to the south of its objective at Trondheim. 'Sickle Force' was sent reinforcements when the British 15th Brigade arrived at Åndalsnes and was rushed into action.

The main problem for all three forces sent to Norway was the chaotic way in which the ships transporting them had been loaded at the docks. Vital heavy equipment and weaponry had been left behind as ships were filled with supplies in no particular order. Halfway to Norway the British units realised that some vital equipment had been left behind at their embarkation port. Shortage of space on the transport ships meant that many of their motor vehicles had also been left behind. One unit of the 148th Brigade had been forced to leave behind half of its personnel and equipment, and landed in Norway with just one truck and three motorcycles!

On 30 April another, much smaller, force (code-named 'Scissors Force'), made up of a battalion of Scots Guards, landed at the port of Bodö, 112 miles to the southwest of Narvik, and directly in the path of a German relief force moving towards the port. Comprising five companies of infantry and two troops of artillery, 'Scissors Force' was under the command of Colonel Colin Gubbins. He was tasked with establishing a base in the region of Bodö in case further Allied troops were sent to Norway.

(**Below**) This soldier is posing on the roof of the *Daily Herald* newspaper in London in early April to model the cold weather clothing of the British Expeditionary Corps going to Norway. In reality this kind of clothing never reached the troops in Norway, largely due to the chaotic circumstances of the expedition. Although some winter hats were issued, the main cold weather items of clothing issued were leather jerkins to be worn over the standard battledress. *(Author's Collection)*

(**Opposite, above**) In what appears to be a relaxed scene, British soldiers chat with the officers of the ship ready to take them to Norway on 20 April. The soldiers belong to the 1/6th Duke of Wellington's Regiment and the ship is the MS *Sobieski*, a Polish merchant ship. The Polish Navy and Polish merchant ships played a major part in the Norwegian Campaign, crewed by men wanting to contribute to the war against Germany. *(Author's Collection)*

(**Opposite, below**) British troops crowd on the decks of the transport ship taking them on a 400-mile journey to Norway. On 15 April an announcement was made by Prime Minister Neville Chamberlain promising the Norwegians that 'help was on its way'. Preparations for the move to Norway were rushed and not always well organised but speed was of the essence. *(Author's Collection)*

The Royal Navy sloop HMS *Bittern* was one of the escorting ships for the Allied transport ships moving along the Norwegian coast. On 30 April the ship was on station near the port of Namsos, protecting shipping from the threat of U-boat attacks, when she was spotted by a squadron of Ju 87/R Stukas. She came under repeated attacks and was heavily damaged. Her crew were taken off by other Allied ships and then *Bittern* was sunk by a torpedo from the Royal Navy destroyer HMS *Janus*. (Author's Collection)

Smiling British soldiers stand on the deck of their transport ship holding the winter coats issued to them to wear along with their greatcoats. These 'tropal' coats were very heavy and were described as being ungainly and stiff to wear. In reality these coats were not widely worn in Norway but sheepskin jerkins were widely worn along with the battledress. (Cody Images)

British troops patiently wait at the Scottish port of Gourock on 20 April to be transported to Norway aboard the Polish liner SS *Sobieski*, which had been in Argentina when the Germans invaded Poland in September 1939. Like other Polish ships, the liner was pressed into Allied service, with several such ships acting as troop transports. (Author's Collection)

British troops stand on the deck of their transport ship which is ready to take them to Norway in April 1940. The soldiers are wearing standard 1937 issue British battledress, which was sufficient for fighting in temperate climates. Some of the winter clothing that was later issued to troops in Norway comprised leftovers from the British Army's intervention in Siberia during the Russian Civil War in 1918–1919. (Author's Collection)

(**Opposite, above**) The surviving crew of the destroyer HMS *Hardy* are being inspected by the then First Lord of the Admiralty Winston Churchill after their return from Norway. Thirty-two of *Hardy*'s crew were killed, including the commander of the destroyer flotilla, Captain Warburton-Lee. The survivors swam ashore and were looked after by the Norwegians until they could be returned to Britain. Most of the men are wearing donated civilian clothing, and several are wearing typical Norwegian caps. Within weeks Churchill would take over from Neville Chamberlain as the British prime minister and would lead Britain to victory. (*Author's Collection*)

(**Above**) In the first days of May a unit of French Chasseurs D'Alpins 'Blue Devils' watch from the deck as they prepare to sail for Norway. The French contribution to the campaign was planned to consist of 25,000 troops, 1,200 pack animals, 1,700 vehicles, 170 guns and 12,000 tons of supplies. The men and equipment were routed between the French port of Brest and the improvised base at Greenock between 8 April and 8 May. There was, however, only enough time to send 15,000 troops to Norway before the expedition was cancelled. (*Author's Collection*)

(**Opposite, below**) During the embarkation of French troops onto their ships to take them to Norway there was time for photo opportunities. The Chasseurs were elite mountain troops, trained for the kind of fighting they were expected to see in Norway, and were the French equivalent of the German Gebirgsjagers. These Chasseurs D'Alpins seem happy to pose and show off their equipment for the news cameraman. Unfortunately the French mountain troops arrived in Norway without a vital piece of equipment: a strap for their skis. Perhaps the photographs should have been curtailed so that these troops could make a final equipment check before they boarded their four troopships. (*Author's Collection*)

Two soldiers from one of the Polish brigades sent to Norway sit on the dockside and discuss the coming campaign in early May. Many Polish men who escaped from Poland in September 1939 were determined to continue the fight against Nazi Germany. They joined brigades set up in France to allow them to serve alongside their fellow countrymen. Although the Poles were described as mountain troops, most of them had not fought in this role during their service in the Polish Army in 1939. (*Author's Collection*)

While they wait for their troopship to be loaded, a group of French soldiers and sailors take part in an impromptu sing-along. While these men were serving in Norway, their comrades were beginning the defence of their mother country from the German invasion. The morale of the French contingent of the expeditionary corps was higher than that in the majority of their army. This was largely because the men who took part were all from elite units such as the Foreign Legion and Chasseurs D'Alpins. Poles fighting in the French Army had the added incentive that they were trying to liberate their country from a brutal occupation. (*Author's Collection*)

Chasseurs D'Alpins milling about on the quay of their embarkation port with their personnel equipment arranged in neat piles. It was not surprising that a large part of the French contingent of the Expeditionary Corps should be made up of these troops. It was the lack of heavy equipment and weaponry that weakened the Allied war effort in Norway, rather than any lack of quality in the troops who fought there. (Author's Collection)

Three Chasseurs D'Alpins 'Blue Devils' take a last look at their homeland before setting off to Norway, with one holding a Saint Bernard puppy mascot. The Chasseurs were trained to operate in mountainous terrain and were ideal troops to be sent to Norway. Most of these troops were destined for Narvik, where they were to support Gubbins' small British force around the port. Some were to join the British in central Norway, reinforcing Maurice Force, which had landed at Namsos. These troops were split between the various British-led forces, with the 5e Demi-Brigade being attached to Maurice Force. Rupert Force at Narvik included the 27e Demi-Brigade, as well as a Demi-Brigade of Foreign Legionnaires. (Author's Collection)

The French Navy Vauquelin-class destroyer *Le Chevalier Paul* was sent as part of their contribution to the naval campaign off Norway. In early May the ship, along with two other destroyers of the same class, was sent to Scotland in preparation for supporting the Allies in Norway. The three ships escorted two French troop convoys to Harstad and Namsos. A sister ship of *Le Chevalier Paul*, *Maille Breze* was lost on 30 April after an accident at a port in Scotland. (Author's Collection)

Well dressed and equipped French troops queue to climb the gangplank of a transport ship. The uniforms issued to the troops going to Norway were not always adequate, with different units having various elements of winter clothing. These men have the anorak-type jackets that were issued to Chasseurs D'Alpins at the start of the campaign. They are all armed with the MAS 1936 rifle, the latest type in service with the French Army in 1940.
(Author's Collection)

French Chasseurs D'Alpins climb the gangplank of their transport ship in the rain carrying their own kit. Stacked up on the dock are other kit bags carrying extra gear for the coming campaign in Norway. The loading of both French and Royal Navy ships was often poorly organised and much of the vital equipment needed by the Allied troops was left behind.
(Author's Collection)

General Bethouard, commander of the French Expeditionary Corps in Scandinavia, is seen onboard a transport ship taking his troops to Norway. He is in conversation with Lieutenant Colonel Magrin-Vernerey (with his back to the camera), who was the commander of the 13th Demi-Brigade of the Foreign Legion (13e DBLE). Magrin-Vernerey was to command his unit in the fighting for Narvik in May 1940. (*Author's Collection*)

Soldiers of the Polish Brigade stand on the deck of their transport ship listening to a 'pep talk' from their officer. Serving in the Polish Army in Exile was an option for the 35,000 Poles who escaped to France in the aftermath of the fall of their country in September 1939. Their unit, named the Podhale Brigade, was also known as the 1st Independent Highland Brigade, with some men serving in it coming originally from the Carpathian Mountains. Others had no experience in mountain warfare but were sent to bulk out the Highland Brigade ranks. On the front of their khaki berets the Poles wore a Polish Eagle cloth badge to show their allegiance to their mother country. (*Author's Collection*)

French troops en route to Norway test their anti-tank gun by firing rounds out to sea from the deck of their transport ship. They are firing a 25mm Canon Leger de 25 SA-L Mle 1937, which was the most potent French anti-tank gun available in April 1940. This was a slightly improved version of the original 1934 gun, which remained in French service in 1940. The crewmen are wearing the M26 steel helmet, which was a slightly improved version of the original Adrian M1915. *(Author's Collection)*

Chapter Eight

Lillehammer

As the Kampfgruppe Pellengahr moved northwards up the Gudbrandsal valley in mid-April they closed in on the strategic town of Lillehammer. Reaching the frozen Lake Mjøsa just to the south of Lillehammer, the Germans split their forces to attack along both shores. As the Germans advanced towards Lillehammer, the defence put up by the Norwegians began to stiffen. In addition, the terrain and snowy conditions caused some short-term delays to the German advance. They were faced by elements of the Norwegian 5th Regiment on the eastern shore and by a single battalion of the 4th Infantry Regiment on the western shore. Both Norwegian units were already demoralised and the situation was not helped when German units outflanked their positions, crossing the frozen lake to outflank first one Norwegian unit and then the other. As both Norwegian units pulled back in disarray, they were joined at the front by units of the British 148th Brigade, diverted from their original objective – the port of Trondheim – at the request of the Norwegian commander-in-chief, General Ruge. Most of the British troops arrived at the front by train along the still intact railway north of Lillehammer. Two companies of Sherwood Foresters deployed along the western shore of the lake while the rest went to relieve the Norwegian units still defending the town. A similar sized force of the Leicestershire Regiment took up positions on the eastern shore, with support from Norwegian dragoons. Advancing towards them were two German infantry battalions and two companies of motorised machine gunners. This force was supported by six light and two heavy tanks and a number of 105mm field guns. On the Allied side there were no tanks or artillery, not even mortars, and most of the British troops were unseasoned. Once the German attack began on 21 April, there was little the Allied troops could do, especially as they were under attack by eight Heinkel III bombers. Although two more companies of the Leicestershire Regiment arrived during the battle, there was little that they could do to prevent the impending defeat. The Allied forces were driven back to their former headquarters at Tretten, where they made a last stand on the 23rd. Under the cover of darkness the remnants of the British and Norwegian forces made a hasty retreat. Left dead on the battlefield or taken prisoner were 706 officers and men. The 148th Brigade now ceased to exist as a fighting unit. The Germans continued their northwards advance as more British troops were being landed in Norway to try to prevent the takeover of central Norway.

German troops march along a country road as they advance northwards from Oslo to join up with their garrisons at a number of towns and cities. Although they held the ports of Bergen, Kristiansand and Narvik as well as the capital, the German hold on Norway was still precarious. Their only opposition in mid-April came from Norwegian units still fighting but the arrival of French and British troops would increase the tempo of the war. (Author's Collection)

A horse-drawn German field gun moves forward on the road to Lillehammer, which according to the sign is 50km (31 miles) away. As the advance went on, the threat of Allied intervention increased, with 'Sickle Force' moving southwards from the port of Åndalsnes. From late April there would be clashes between combined British and Norwegian troops and the Germans. The British troops had left their base on the 20th and advanced at speed to take on the enemy in the Lillehammer region. (Author's Collection)

As the German Army moved through southern and central Norway they utilised every method of transport they could find. This unit has requisitioned a civilian truck, while one of their comrades tries to ride a bicycle over the icy road. Most German victories in Norway were won by using proactive tactics, not by force of arms. The Germans had tanks and artillery in Norway but not in great numbers and it was their skill in using what they had to good effect that eventually won them their victory. *(Author's Collection)*

British troops march out of their forward base at Tretten station, a railway junction a short distance from Lillehammer. Here they were ordered to wait for the arrival of the main German force moving northwards. These men belong to D Company of the 1/5th Battalion, Leicestershire Regiment and are headed to the front. They would soon clash with the German Army to the north of Lillehammer. *(Joseph Kynoch)*

This propaganda photograph from the German magazine *Signal* shows a machine gun squad moving through a town in central Norway. Following on from the military victory against Poland in September, the conquest of Denmark and Norway further served to prove German superiority. *(Author's Collection)*

(**Opposite, above**) British troops rest on the road to Lillehammer. The trucks were provided by the Norwegians to transport their Canon Leger de 25 antichar SA-L Mle 1934 anti-tank guns, which had been sold by the French to the British in 1939 to fill the gap due to shortage of home-produced British 2-pounder guns. When the British tried to tow these guns behind trucks they found that they were too flimsy and instead they had to be transported on lorries. These guns were to destroy a number of German light tanks and scout cars, with their 0.7lb shells being capable of penetrating their armour. Some Norwegian officers were disappointed by the British soldiers, especially the Territorials who made up the 146th and 148th Brigades. One described the Territorials disparagingly as 'untrained steel workers from the Midlands'. *(Author's Collection)*

(**Opposite, below**) One of the trio of heavy tanks sent to Norway in mid-April is seen moving through the outskirts of Lillehammer. These experimental tanks were not supposed to see service in the war but were sent as an emergency reinforcement to Norway. Two of them were kept on the strength of Pz.Abt.z.B.v.40 while the third was attached to the Kampfgruppe Pellengahr. These tanks were based on a number of super-heavy tanks being developed by France, Britain and the Soviet Union. *(Author's Collection)*

(**Opposite, above**) German troops hunch over as they move forward behind a Panzer I light tank. This photograph, taken during the fighting around Lillehammer in late April, shows the relatively small size of this tank. Its armament comprised only two light machine guns in the turret and its role was purely as an infantry support tank. (*Author's Collection*)

(**Opposite, below**) With the burning buildings of Lillehammer behind them, a platoon of Germans gather around a Panzer I light tank. The protection given by the tank's armour was minimal for its size, and provided little cover from small arms fire. During their final advance on the town they had been faced by two organised groups of Norwegians totalling several thousand. These troops were, however, totally exhausted and were increasingly overwhelmed by the superior weaponry of the German attackers. (*Author's Collection*)

(**Above**) German troops move tentatively through a village near Lillehammer on 21 April. Fighting for the town involved Norwegian troops and the 148th Brigade of the British Army's 'Sickle Force'. British troops made up of the 8th Battalion, Sherwood Foresters and the 5th Leicesters took up positions to the south of the town in an open valley. Their main objective was to hold off the superior German force until their Norwegian Allies could withdraw safely. (*Author's Collection*)

Disconsolate British troops gathered in the centre of Lillehammer after their defeat. The British troops who were shipped to Norway lacked equipment and heavy weaponry. They were facing the comparatively well organised Germany Army in central Norway (though some Wehrmacht units were also short of weapons). The Germans had superiority in tanks, artillery, machine guns and, vitally, air support during the campaign. The haste with which the military expedition was organised frequently led to mix-ups and vital weaponry being left behind. The sinking of transport ships with heavy equipment aboard did not help the chaotic situation. (Author's Collection)

(**Opposite, above**) German soldiers protect themselves from the heat of the fire as houses on the outskirts of Lillehammer burn fiercely. They are facing a combined force of Norwegians, who had been fighting for over a week against their advance, and newly arrived British troops. It was a one-sided fight, with the lightly armed Allied units having to deal with Germans supported by artillery and the ever-present Luftwaffe. (Author's Collection)

(**Opposite, below**) A group of British soldiers marching into captivity, having been taken prisoner in the fighting around the town of Lillehammer. The troops are wearing a variety of uniforms, with one soldier wearing the new winter uniform issued for service in Norway. At the front of the group several soldiers are wearing brown leather jerkins with their khaki battledress. After several British defeats troops were reported to be wandering around the Norwegian countryside looking for German troops to take them prisoner. With nothing to eat and nowhere to go, the soldiers had little choice but to look for the safety of captivity. (Author's Collection)

The photographs of surrendered British troops at Lillehammer were widely circulated around the world by the Nazi press. These young soldiers were captured during the day-long struggle for the town on 22 April. The Norwegian troops who had been defending the town were low on morale and ammunition, and their commander-in-chief, General Ruge, asked for help from the newly arrived British. Two companies of the 1st Battalion, 8th Sherwood Foresters were rushed by train to confront the advancing Germans. When the British arrived to the north of Lillehammer, they found that the Norwegians were withdrawing in front of a strong German force. Decisively, the Germans had six light and two heavy tanks, which the British could not match, and by the end of the 22nd the Allies were withdrawing from the town. (Author's Collection)

A Panzer II light tank of *Panzer Abteilung zur besonderer Vervendung* 40 driving through a town in central Norway. These tanks were more potent than the Panzer I, with a 20mm main turret gun instead of the machine guns of the earlier model. On 20 April two companies arrived in Norway from Denmark, with seven Panzer IIs in each unit. In total fifteen Panzer II tanks arrived in Norway during the campaign, and in the later weeks of the war they played a decisive role. (Author's Collection)

Chapter Nine

Air Warfare over Norway

Although the Royal Navy was to totally dominate the seas around Norway during the 1940 campaign, the German Luftwaffe equally dominated the skies above. The German planners knew that their weakness at sea would have to be compensated for by their strength in the air. In total the Germans committed 537 planes to the invasion of Denmark and Norway, including several types of seaplane, Me Bf110 and Me Bf109E fighters and Heinkel 111, Dornier 215 and Junkers 88 medium bombers. Junkers Ju 87R 'Stuka' dive-bombers were to serve the Germans well during the campaign, with their constant ground attacks demoralising the Allied ground forces. Junkers Ju 52/3m transports were the reliable workhorse of the Luftwaffe during the Norwegian Campaign. They flew a total of 3,000 sorties, which included transporting 3,000 German troops. Supplies delivered to Norway by the Junkers totalled 2,370 tons, with 250,000 gallons of fuel also being delivered. It is no exaggeration to say that the Ju 52/3m was the most vital German aircraft during the fighting. They landed troops at strategic points during the early days of the campaign and managed to keep the cut-off German garrison at Narvik supplied during May. The various Luftwaffe medium bombers kept up raids against the British-held ports at Harstad, Namsos and Åndalsnes throughout the campaign. These towns were effectively levelled during the campaign and very few buildings survived the attacks. Junkers Ju 87s concentrated on dive-bombing and strafing Allied naval and ground forces. They attacked shipping off the Norwegian coast, as well as Norwegian, British and French units that were facing German forces.

In the opening stages of the campaign the only Allied air presence over Norway consisted of bombers launching a series of small-scale air raids on German-held ports. The air base at Stavanger was particularly targeted by the RAF, but the number of bombers available for these missions was inadequate. A major problem for the RAF bombing effort was the lack of suitable bombers. At this stage of the war the RAF had to depend on three main types of medium bomber, all developed in the 1930s. These were the Armstrong Whitworth Whitley, and early versions of the Handley Page Hampden and the Vickers Wellington. None of these planes was particularly suitable for long-range bombing, with their maximum range allowing only a short time in Norwegian air-space.

During the invasion a number of Norwegian Air Force Gloster Gladiators took on Me110 fighters over the air base at Fornebau. Although the Norwegian pilots fought bravely they were unable to make much impact and could not stop the Germans from capturing all their objectives. A handful of Norwegian planes were also used in the later fighting in central and southern Norway. These aircraft were either Fokker CV light bombers or Moth trainers, which were used as liaison planes. They spent their service darting around at low level to try to avoid the hundreds of Luftwaffe planes that dominated the air above Norway. Further opposition to the Luftwaffe came with the arrival of RAF fighters in mid-April. The 263rd Squadron's Gloster Gladiators were to operate from the frozen Lake Lesjaskog, but this deployment was a disaster and all the squadron's aircraft were put out of action after three days. The squadron was hastily withdrawn back to Britain but returned to Norway in May, this time being sent further north, where it operated until the final evacuation from Narvik in June. When the 263rd Squadron returned in May it was joined by the 46th Squadron, equipped with Hawker Hurricanes, and based at Bodö and Bardufoss from 26 May. The Hurricanes and Gladiators were flown into Norway from the decks of the two carriers HMS *Glorious* and HMS *Furious* on 23 May. By late May the two depleted RAF fighter squadrons in Norway were struggling to counter the constant Luftwaffe attacks. Operating from their bases at Harstad and Skaanland they flew a total of seventy-five sorties, during which they shot down a large number of German aircraft, especially the bombers that were attacking Norwegian civilian as well as military targets. Nine enemy planes were shot down during one heavy German bombing raid on 1 June. From 22 May until 7 June the Gladiators of the 263rd Squadron shot down twenty-six Luftwaffe planes. The 46th Squadron, with its more lethal but fewer Hurricanes, shot down eleven aircraft during the same period. On the ground the anti-aircraft gunners operating at Harstad were able to bring down twenty-three more aircraft. When the Allied evacuation began, the RAF pilots volunteered to land their valuable planes on the deck of the aircraft carrier HMS *Glorious*, which they successfully achieved. In a cruel twist of fate the pilots and their planes went down with the ship when she was torpedoed by the Kriegsmarine's *Scharnhorst* and *Gneisenau*.

RAF bomber pilots scramble from their dispersal hut to climb aboard their planes as they prepare to set off on a bombing raid over Norway. The Handley Page bombers that this crew flew were renowned for their lack of defensive armament and they suffered heavy losses in daylight raids. As soon as possible the Hampden was restricted to night raids, where they suffered fewer attacks as the Luftwaffe did not have night-fighters early in the war. *(Author's Collection)*

The crew of a Handley Page Hampden HP52 bomber warm up their engines before setting out on a night raid over Norway in early May. During the early stages of the Second World War the Hampden carried much of the load for the RAF bomber force. When the war began there were three main bombers in RAF service, the Hampden, the Whitley and the Wellington. *(Author's Collection)*

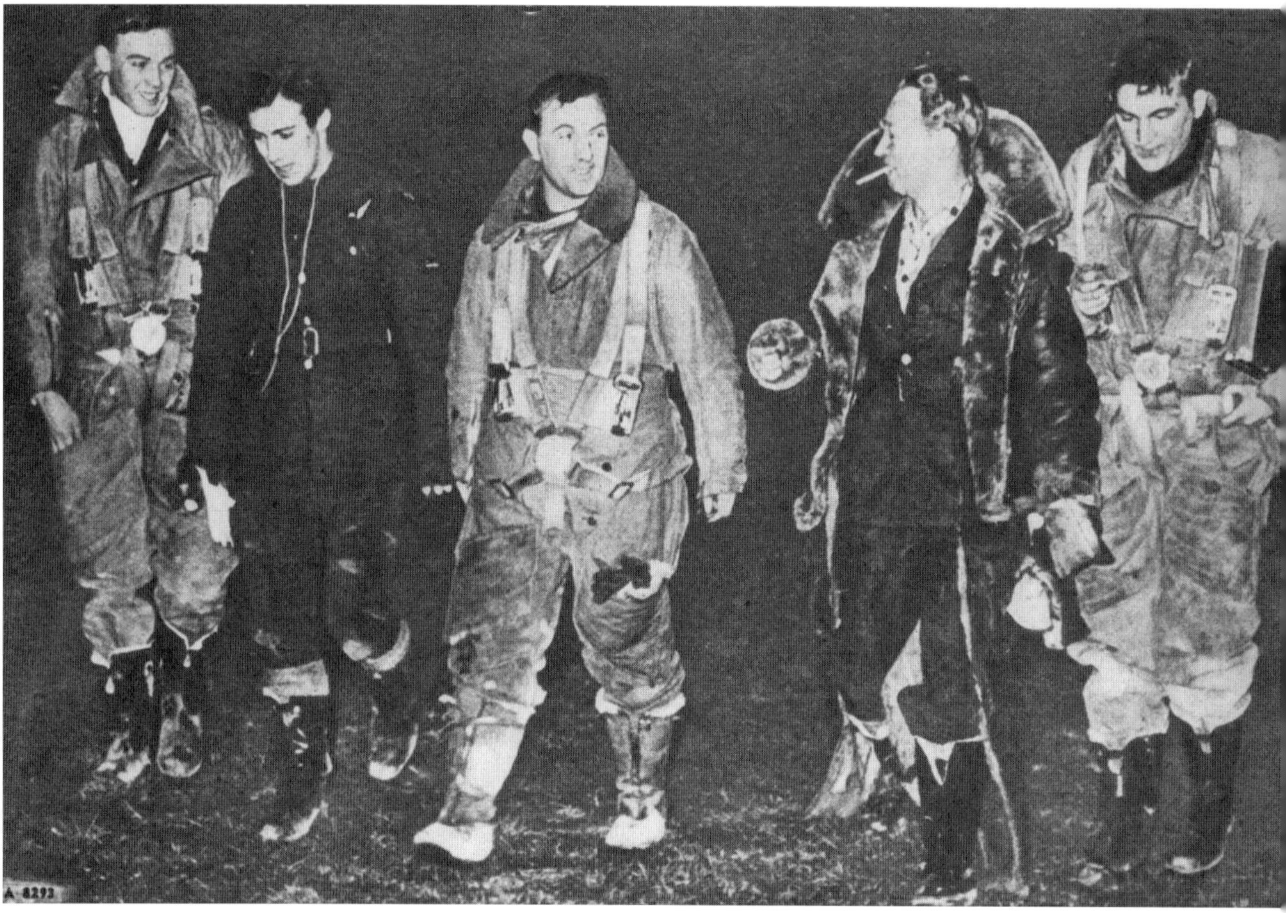
A 8293

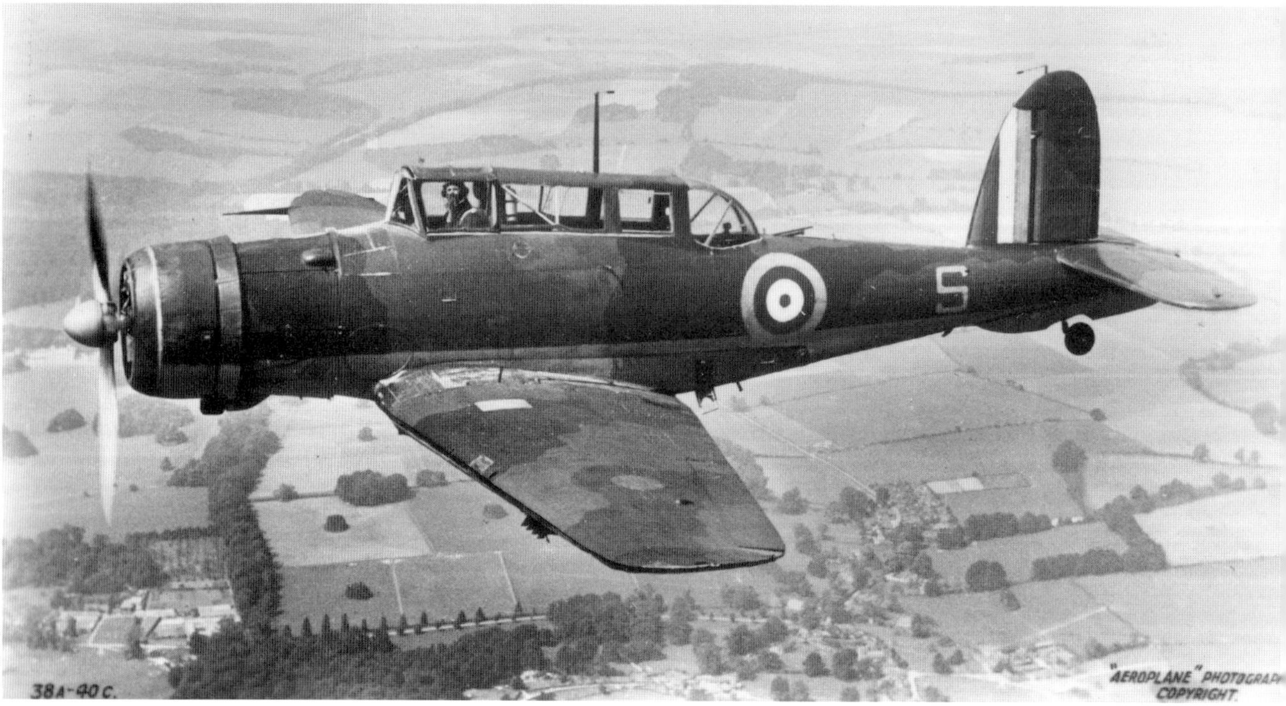
38A-40C.
"AEROPLANE" PHOTOGRAP
COPYRIGHT.

(**Opposite, above**) The five-man crew of an RAF bomber look relaxed having returned to their base from a night raid over Norway in April. According to the caption from a French news magazine, their squadron had made five successive raids on Fornebau airfield at Stavanger. They were said to have used incendiaries and high explosive bombs on the airfield and were reported to have destroyed or damaged several Luftwaffe aircraft. (*Author's Collection*)

(**Opposite, below**) A Fleet Air Arm Blackburn Skua Mk II dive-bomber pictured before the Norwegian Campaign. The Skua was an effective plane that could perform in the fighter role although its main role was as a dive-bomber. The shortage of suitable aircraft was a major issue for the Royal Air Force during the Norwegian Campaign. With only a handful of modern Hurricane fighters and ageing Gloster Gladiators to provide fighter cover for the Allies, the Luftwaffe was able to continue to dominate the skies above Norway. (*Author's Collection*)

(**Above**) This rare photograph from a French magazine shows a Blackburn Skua Mk II dive-bomber of the Fleet Air Arm dropping a couple of bombs on a German ship. Sixteen Skuas of the 800th and 803rd Squadrons of the Royal Naval Air Service sank the German Navy's cruiser *Konigsberg* on 9 April. The Skuas were stationed on an RNAS base on the Orkney Islands and caught the German ship at anchor in Bergen harbour. Although the caption does not say so, this Skua may well be one of the planes that took part in that operation. (*Author's Collection*)

(**Above**) A Blackburn Skua on a frozen lake in Norway is being looked over by French Chasseurs D'Alpins. The Skua was slow, with a top speed of only 225mph, and was already obsolescent when it entered service in 1938. It was armed with .303 machine guns in the wings and another operated at the rear by the observer. Its bombload was a single 500lb bomb carried under the fuselage or eight 30lb bombs mounted beneath the wings. (*Author's Collection*)

(**Opposite, above**) Another view of the Skua Mk II shows the conditions in which its crew had to operate, with snow covering the frozen lake. The plane's folding wings are seen to good effect here. One major problem was that their hydraulic mechanisms were susceptible to freezing at temperatures below −10 °F. The French troops look curiously at the abandoned aircraft, which was one of the few Allied planes in Norway. (*Author's Collection*)

(**Opposite, below**) An RAF Gloster Gladiator of the 263rd Fighter Squadron pictured on the runway of its station at Bardufoss, which regularly came under Luftwaffe attack. This plane, which a few years previously had been the latest type of fighter, was quickly becoming obsolete in the aircraft design frenzy of the late 1930s. It served with the 263rd Squadron, which had eighteen planes operating from the frozen Lake Lesja, but they only survived for two and a half days. During their brief service the lake they operated from was constantly bombed by the Luftwaffe and thirteen Gladiators were hit on the ground. They did manage to down fifteen German planes but the last five Gladiators were set on fire by their crews and the squadron's pilots were evacuated back to Britain to be re-equipped. (*Author's Collection*)

(**Above**) The Luftwaffe crew of a Heinkel He III medium bomber examine a map before going on a bombing raid over Norway. There were six men in a He III crew and these men may have already seen action over Poland in 1939. Their aircraft was the most common type in service with the Luftwaffe over Norway, serving in the bomber role beside Dornier 215s. One disadvantage that the Luftwaffe did have was its crews' habit of keeping strictly to a bombing schedule, allowing the RAF to know when to expect attacks. (*Author's Collection*)

(**Above**) Two Heinkel He III medium bombers are refuelled before going on a mission over Norway in April 1940. These bombers were active over Norway throughout the campaign and were usually free from any enemy fighter activity. The He III, which was known as 'the Spade' by its crews, carried its bombload in vertical racks inside the fuselage. It was the dominant bomber of the Luftwaffe from 1937 until the end of the war, even though it was susceptible to enemy fighters. (*Author's Collection*)

(**Opposite, above**) A Messerschmitt Bf 110 long-range fighter flies over the mountainous terrain of Norway in April 1940. The Bf 110 had a range of 528 miles, compared to the 310-mile range of the Messerschmitt Bf 109 fighter. During the invasion five Bf 110s audaciously landed at Forenbu airfield and managed to hold it until Ju 52s arrived with troops to occupy it. The Bf 110 was susceptible to enemy fighters but in Norway there were too few RAF fighters available to counter it. (*Author's Collection*)

(**Opposite, below**) A Ju 87R Stuka is returning from a bombing mission, having dropped its load on enemy positions. These dive-bombers did not have the range required to operate easily over the wide open spaces of Norway. For this reason there were only forty of these aircraft in Norway, although they saw a lot of action during the two-month campaign. (*Author's Collection*)

A pair of Ju 87R Stuka dive-bombers in flight over Norway returning from a mission. The Stuka was to have its heyday during the fighting of the Blitzkrieg era from September 1939 to May 1941. As the fighter opposition increased, this relatively slow aircraft's weaknesses were exposed, leading to heavy casualties. (*Author's Collection*)

A stack of bombs waiting to be loaded onto the Ju 87R Stuka in the background ready for the next ground-attack mission against Allied ground and naval forces. They are 250kg bombs, which were carried under the fuselage of the Stuka, and there were usually two 50kg bombs under each wing. (*Author's Collection*)

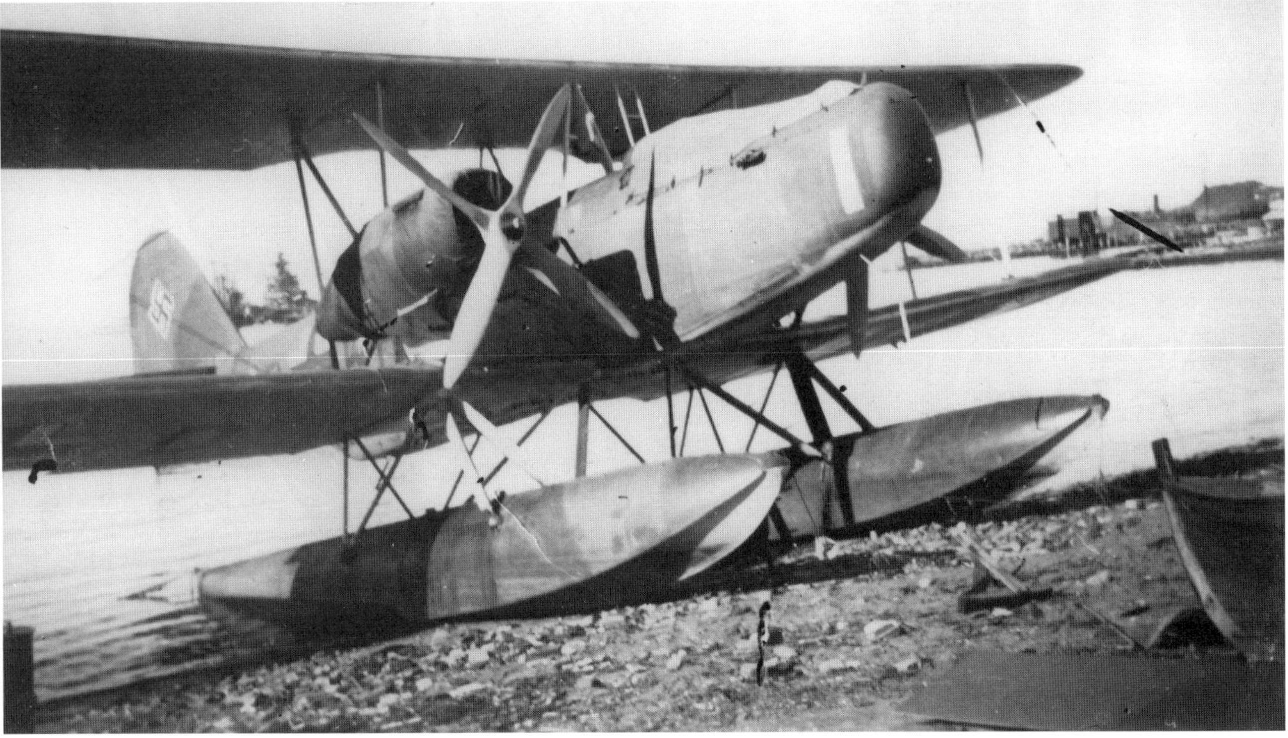

A Heinkel He59 seaplane sits beached on the bank of a fjord during the Norwegian Campaign. This plane was one of the few new aircraft which had been built before Hitler came to power. Besides acting as a reconnaissance and light bombing plane, the He59's main role was as a minelayer. *(Author's Collection)*

Luftwaffe pilots gather around one of their Me109E fighters at Sola airfield at the port of Stavanger. A single Group of Me109s was sent to Norway to defend captured airfields and bases from Allied air attacks. The lack of RAF fighter opposition during the campaign meant that the German fighters assigned in April 1940 did not really need to be reinforced. *(Author's Collection)*

A Luftwaffe Dornier Do215B medium bomber flies over Norway on one of the many raids against Allied-held towns and cities. This updated version of the Dornier 17 bomber was 70mph faster and could carry an additional 500lb bombload. The Luftwaffe's total superiority in the air compensated to a large degree for the Kriegsmarine's inferiority during the campaign. *(Author's Collection)*

A cluster of bombs photographed dropping from an RAF bomber onto the German-controlled airfield at Stavanger. The air base at Stavanger was the best in Norway and vital to the supply system of the German Army. It was used to bring in more troops to reinforce the limited number of German troops in the country. Any effort that the RAF could make to disrupt its use might help their ground forces when they arrived in Norway. *(Author's Collection)*

An RAF reconnaissance mission over the German air base at Stavanger shows planes that were targeted in a bombing raid. According to contemporary records, the raids on this Norwegian port began on 10 April, with a single plane attacking in the morning and later in the day two planes dropping bombs. The following day a total of nine bombers attacked Stavanger in two raids and over the next week there was a series of seven raids involving a total of forty-one bombers. Some raids involved only a single aircraft, while the largest two raids on 15 April were made up of nine bombers each. These raids did a lot of damage and destroyed a number of Luftwaffe aircraft and facilities but the base remained operational. (*Author's Collection*)

(**Above**) This photograph shows bombs dropping from an RAF bomber onto the port of Bergen in early May. Although the RAF was short of bombers with sufficient range to reach Norway, some raids were launched. On 9 April a raid by twelve Armstrong Whitworth Whitley bombers had taken place over Bergen, with the targets being Kriegsmarine ships getting ready to return to Germany. No conclusive hits on the shipping in the harbour were reported by the Whitleys, but there were a number of near-misses. The bombers returned to base having lost one of their number during the raid and with little to show for their operation. (*Author's Collection*)

(**Opposite, above**) A pair of Lockheed Hudson A28 bombers flying 50ft above sea level during a mission to Norway. The Hudson, the first US-made plane to fly with the RAF, entered service with RAF squadrons in 1938 and saw service over Norway in 1940. It was a Hudson flying in the reconnaissance role that discovered the position of the German ship *Altmark* in February. Another RAF Hudson guided HMS *Cossack* to the fjord where *Altmark* was hiding and pinpointed her location. (*Author's Collection*)

(**Opposite, below**) The crew of a Lockheed Hudson A28 marine bomber/reconnaissance plane examining the damage to one of the plane's wings which it had suffered during its latest mission to Norway. Hudsons remained in service with the RAF until 1945 as new versions of the original were developed. (*Author's Collection*)

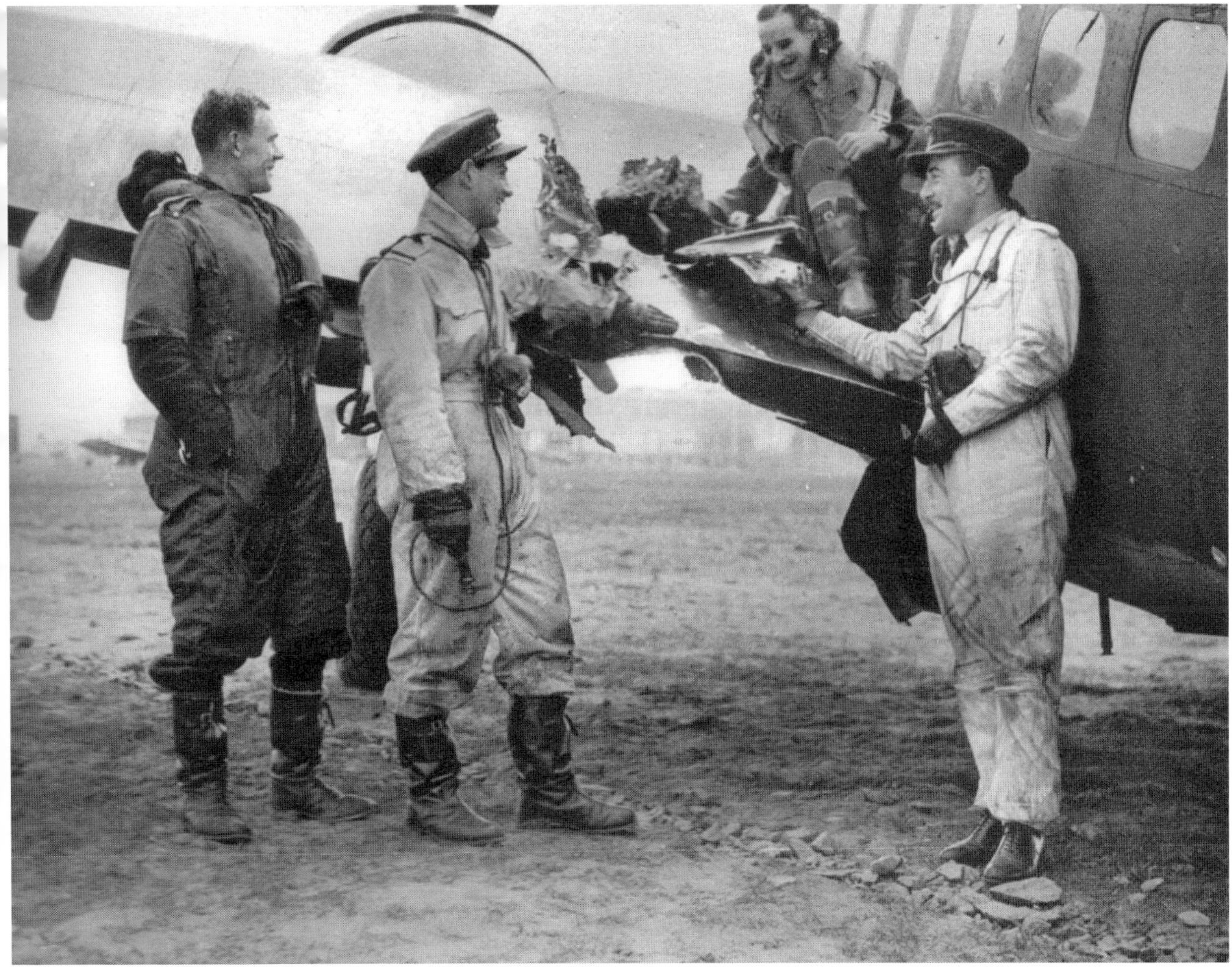

Another Hudson A28 crew chatting before setting off on a reconnaissance mission over Norway in May 1940. The crew are (*from left to right*) the navigator, the pilot, the wireless operator and the rear gunner. In the basket carried by the rear gunner are carrier pigeons, which were carried by the bomber in case the wireless failed during a mission.

Chapter Ten

Allied Failures in Central Norway

The landing of 6,000 Allied troops at the ports of Namsos on 16 April and at Åndalsnes on the 18th marked the beginning of an ill-fated attempt to support the Norwegian Army in central Norway. Both brigades arrived in a disorganised state, with much of their heavy equipment and weaponry missing. Tanks, artillery and anti-aircraft guns were not unloaded owing to constant Luftwaffe raids or were lost when the ships transporting them were sunk. In effect, the 146th Brigade ('Maurice Force') which arrived at Namsos and the 148th Brigade ('Sickle Force') at Åndalsnes were poorly armed infantry formations. Without heavy machine guns, mortars and artillery, most units only had Lee Enfield .303 rifles and Bren guns! When French troops arrived to reinforce the 146th and the British 15th Brigade arrived to reinforce the 148th they did bring small amounts of artillery with them. Regardless of these problems, Maurice Force and Sickle Force were given the joint objective of taking the German-held port of Trondheim. The 146th Brigade was to advance southwards from Namsos to Trondheim, while the 148th Brigade was to move northwards from Åndalsnes towards the port. Allied forces in central Norway now outnumbered the 1,800-strong Trondheim garrison by 2 to 1, causing Hitler to panic. He ordered an immediate reinforcement of the port, which by 30 April had received 5,500 extra troops. These reinforcements had been flown into Vaernes airfield by Ju 52/3m transports with the protection of Luftwaffe fighters.

Almost immediately the critical situation in central Norway led to the 148th Brigade being ordered eastwards to Lillehammer, where the Norwegians were struggling to halt the advance of a German Kampfgruppe moving up from Oslo (see Chapter 9). General Ruge had begged for Allied support for his troops, saying that his men were 'near to exhaustion'. Meanwhile the 146th Brigade continued its advance southwards and soon clashed with a strong force of German troops moving north from Trondheim. By the 16th the Germans had reached the strategic town of Verdal. There, waiting, was a small force of eighty Norwegian troops, along with a few Royal Engineers sent to the town to repair a bridge. In the subsequent one-sided battle the Germans, well armed with mortars and light artillery, pushed the Allied troops back.

Much of the fighting took place around the village of Vist on the 23rd and 24th, with the defeated British and French having to fall back to their headquarters further north at Steinkjer. This small town had been under heavy Luftwaffe attack, with 242 houses destroyed and its 1,800 population homeless. As the Allies withdrew towards Namsos, a Norwegian force was left to hold back the advancing Germans at Steinkjer. By the end of April it had been decided to evacuate Maurice Force from Namsos, beginning on 1 May. The evacuation was completed by the 3rd.

Meanwhile the 148th Brigade, reinforced by the 15th Brigade, was withdrawing from the area around Lillehammer leaving behind a number of prisoners. The weary troops now faced a 140-mile retreat back up the Gudbrandsdal valley after being pushed out of Lillehammer on 22 April. During this withdrawal the 15th Brigade fought a rearguard action at Kvam on 24 April. A column of motorised German troops attacked dug-in British troops of the King's Own Yorkshire Light Infantry equipped with two Hotchkiss guns. The Germans were led by one of the giant 35-ton NbFz tanks, which was disabled by an anti-tank round. A Panzer II light tank was also hit by a 25mm shell and put out of action, while an SdFfz 231 scout car retreated from the battle. After this rare success for the Allies the majority of Sickle Force continued the retreat to Åndalsnes, coming under regular attack from the Luftwaffe before reaching the port in time to be evacuated. By 2 May Sickle Force had been evacuated, leaving their angry Norwegian allies to continue the hopeless fight. The Allied intervention in central Norway had ended in almost complete failure. The Allied planners now decided that the only place worth fighting for was the northern port of Narvik.

The commanding officer at Namsos, General Adrian Paul Ghislain Carton de Wiart VC, KBE, CB, CMG, DSO was a brave officer of Belgian and Irish parents. He served in the Boer War and the First World War, and tunnelled out of a prisoner-of-war camp. According to his biography he had been shot in the face, head, stomach, ankle, leg, hip and ear, and had been blinded in his left eye. In addition he had survived two plane crashes and tore off his own fingers when a doctor refused to amputate them! In April 1940 he was given the command of the 146th Brigade sent to Namsos and was highly critical of the chaotic organisation of the Norwegian Campaign. He is seen here at his sparse headquarters at Namsos with his ADC before the port was levelled to the ground by Luftwaffe bombing raids.
(Author's Collection)

British and Norwegian troops of Maurice Force prepare to move southwards from Namsos in late April towards their main objective: the port of Trondheim. These British troops are riding in the back of a Norwegian civilian truck, which is being driven by its owner. Unfortunately most Norwegians did not speak English and of course the troops did not speak Norwegian. When the British arrived at Åndalsnes they had no detailed maps of the region as they had originally been earmarked to land at Namsos. (*Author's Collection*)

(**Opposite, above**) Cheerful British troops on their way to the front on a civilian truck. The advance of the two British task forces from the ports of Namsos and Åndalsnes were both aimed at the German-held port of Trondheim. In the early stages of the British advances there was some optimism amongst the Allied troops. However, their morale was to suffer some heavy blows when they were confronted by the advancing German armoured columns. (Author's Collection)

(**Above**) In this highly symbolic photograph a French Chasseur D'Alpin, a Norwegian and a British infantryman pose at the side of the road. The British soldier belongs to the 146th Brigade Maurice Force which landed at the port of Namsos on 16 April. On the same day the French 5th Chasseurs D'Alpins Demi-Brigade was landed to act as support for the British. Their unarmed Norwegian comrade belongs to one of the units that continued to resist the German invasion. Norwegian commanders were relieved to see the Allied support arriving in mid-April but it was reported that the Norwegians were disappointed by the size of the military intervention by the Allies and their lack of heavy weaponry. (Author's Collection)

(**Opposite, below**) A British soldier drives a Ford light truck during the advance towards Trondheim in mid-April. Because most of the British transport had been left behind, the British often relied on donated Norwegian civilian vehicles. Although these vehicles certainly helped with the Allies' transport difficulties, there was also a shortage of heavy weaponry and equipment. (Author's Collection)

French reinforcements landed at the port of Namsos on 19 April to support the British offensive. Their disembarkation was made under heavy enemy air attack and vital equipment was left on the ships that had brought them to Norway. Two battalions of Chasseurs D'Alpins had to leave some of their ski gear on the ships, along with the mules they depended on for transport. Most of the French troops did not leave Namsos and had to endure constant Luftwaffe bombing raids while trying to organise the rear area for the coming campaign. Here French troops try to repair the telephone lines which had been damaged during one of the air raids. *(Author's Collection)*

A friendly Norwegian farmer lends a hand to a British anti-aircraft crew to move their 40mm Bofors gun into position near Namsos. This photograph perhaps typifies the situation in central Norway for the Allied forces. There were some artillery tractors available in Norway but they were few and far between in 1940. Some of these Bofors guns had also unfortunately been unloaded at the disembarkation port without their predictors, which made accurate aiming extremely difficult. (Author's Collection)

Four Norwegian riflemen defend the town of Steinkjer on 18 April in support of the British 146th Brigade. The Allied advance from Namsos ended at the town and within a few days the British and French were withdrawing back to the port they had set out from. Although the Norwegians still fighting the German invaders had been pleased to have the support of the Franco-British forces, the failure of the Allies to combat the enemy effectively was a great disappointment to them. (Author's Collection)

(**Opposite, above**) This close-up of a Norwegian M29 machine gun shows the kind of conditions faced by the combatants in 1940. The main advantage that the Norwegians had during the fighting was their familiarity with the terrain in which they were fighting. In addition units were raised and expanded during the campaign using local volunteers who knew the countryside well. (*Author's Collection*)

(**Opposite, below**) A Norwegian Colt-Browning M29 heavy machine gun team fire from their forest position in support of the British 146th Brigade. As British troops were withdrawn to Namsos ready for their evacuation, they were told not to inform the Norwegians fighting nearby. This order came from the top and it was not until 2 May that the British commanders informed Colonel Getz of their plans. They left behind a few crates of rifles with notes to the Norwegian troops saying 'hope you can use these'. (*Author's Collection*)

(**Above**) British sentries of the 146th Brigade man a checkpoint on the main Namsos-Steinkjer road. The town of Steinkjer was along the main road south towards the Allied objective of Trondheim. Heavy Luftwaffe bombing destroyed most of the stores of the brigade's forward base at Steinkjer on 21 April. Faced by increasing German strength, it was decided to withdraw the 146th northwards to their main base at Namsos. As the British withdrew from their positions at Steinkjer, they relied on units of the Norwegian 13th Regiment to cover them. (*Author's Collection*)

(**Above**) Norwegian troops of the 13th Regiment setting up a bivouac in the forests close to Lake Snaasa during their advance towards the town of Steinkjer in late April. These men were under the command of Colonel Getz, who was unaware that at this time the Allies were withdrawing back to the port of Namsos. He agreed on 26 April to begin an attack on Steinkjer but did not know that the British troops on his flanks were being gradually withdrawn. (Author's Collection)

(**Opposite, above**) These British troops, escorted by a single German soldier, are reported to have been taken prisoner in the region of Steinkjer on 21 April. The Allies' original plan to capture this vital port was that a British force ('Hammer Force') would be landed on the coast nearby. This plan was abandoned and British troops were landed only at Namsos and Åndalsnes with the intention that the two forces would attack Trondheim from north and south. The final plan was for a pincer movement to be organised to take the port but this plan was abandoned on 20 April. There was a shortage of both troops and heavy weaponry, and by this stage the Norwegian troops were totally exhausted. (Author's Collection)

(**Opposite, below**) Norwegian prisoners of war repairing roads in the region of Namsos for their German captors, although strictly speaking, making prisoners do manual work was against the rules of the Geneva Convention. These soldiers of the 13th Regiment had been the first to face the advance of the German 138th Mountain and 359th Infantry Regiments. The 13th was the only Norwegian unit that fought alongside the British troops who were part of Maurice Force. (Author's Collection)

(**Above**) A girl shelters under a tree on the outskirts of the port of Namsos to avoid the bombing of her town. Norwegian civilians suffered greatly during the campaign, largely due to the indiscriminate bombing by the Luftwaffe. When British and French troops landed at Namsos they quickly moved out of the town to try to prevent it being targeted by the Germans. This did not work, however, and most of the small town and the port facilities were flattened by German bombers; the town virtually ceased to exist. (*Author's Collection*)

(**Opposite, above**) British troops pick through the debris of the ruined port of Namsos after a devastating Luftwaffe bombing raid on 20 April. Namsos was the headquarters of the British Army in central Norway and troops who were landed at the port were soon advancing in all directions. They joined up with Norwegian units under the command of Colonel Getz and clashed with German forces. Of course the fact that the British forces were stationed there made Namsos a prime target for German bombing raids during mid-April. (*Author's Collection*)

(**Opposite, below**) A British signalman in Namsos has stripped down his radio as he tries to get his damaged apparatus working. British commanders complained about the poor reliability of their unit radios during the campaign. Some of the fragile radios had been broken in transit and others arrived with parts missing as they had not been packed carefully at embarkation. (*Author's Collection*)

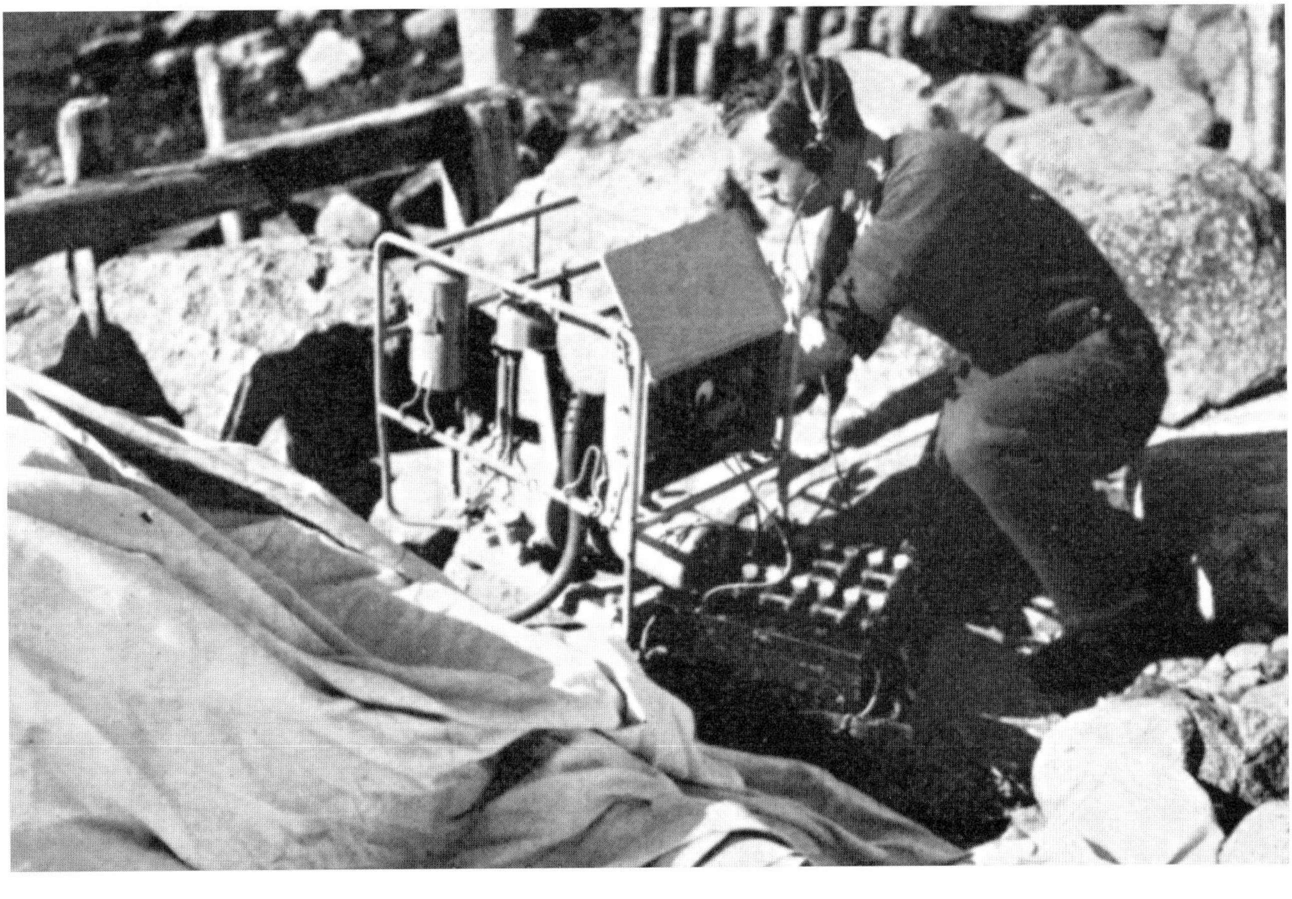

King Haakon VII and his son the Crown Prince and future King Olav V pictured in officers' uniforms in late April. The two royals were moved from Oslo to Hamar, where the king received a message from the Germans offering a ceasefire. He refused the offer and the royal party moved to Nybergsund, where they were attacked by a German force. They were then evacuated to Trondheim before leaving Norway at the end of the campaign. In a speech intended to encourage continued resistance against the Germans, King Haakon said: 'Comrades in arms of all nations fighting at the front in Northern Norway: remain stubborn in battle and strong in your conviction that the good cause will be victorious in the end.' (*Author's Collection*)

Chapter Eleven

The Fighting in Northern Norway, 8 May–1 June

By early May the German Army had advanced through southern and central Norway and some units were now moving into the northern region of Nordland. Their main objective was to move to the far north and to relieve the threatened German garrison at the port of Narvik. Secondary objectives included establishing airfields in Nordland to make supplying Narvik easier. In an attempt to stop this German advance small units of British and French ski troops were sent to the southern part of Nordland. A much larger force of British and Norwegian troops was in position in central and northern Nordland by the middle of May.

In an attempt to adapt to the conditions in Norway, the British War Office established in Britain ten independent companies that were trained to launch raids on the German Army as it advanced through Nordland. Four of the companies were ready to go to Norway by late April and were formed into a unit called 'Scissor Force'. Under the command of Lieutenant Colonel Gubbins, they landed at the port of Bodö and then established defences at the towns of Mo i Rana and Mosjoen.

When the Germans reached the first of these towns, Mosjoen, on 5 May they faced 400 Norwegians defenders, who were reinforced by the British 4th and 5th Independent Companies on 8 May, just in time for the Germans to push them out of the town. On 9 May the British 24th Guards Brigade was sent by sea from its positions around Narvik to reinforce the positions in Nordland. The urgent British redeployments were to include the Irish Guards and three light tanks of the 3rd King's Own Hussars. A series of disasters at sea scuppered the reinforcement, with the Irish Guards' ship MS *Chrobry* being sunk and taking a number of guardsmen with her. Some 700 survivors were taken back to Harstad near Narvik to be re-equipped before returning to Nordland. On 17 May the Royal Navy cruiser HMS *Effingham* ran aground with the 2nd Battalion, South Wales Borderers aboard. They also had to be taken back to Harstad without most of their equipment, although three Bren gun carriers were later salvaged from the wreck.

While the British were suffering these setbacks, the Germans maintained their advance, moving northwards from Mosjoen to Mo i Rana. By the 17th the Germans were fighting the British force stationed at the town, which was made up of the 1st Scots Guards Battalion, the 1st Independent Company, four 25-pounder field guns and a few 40mm Bofors anti-aircraft guns. The German attacking force was made up of the 2nd Battalion, 137th Mountain Regiment, which launched a frontal attack. Meanwhile a flanking force of German ski troops caused panic in the British ranks and their withdrawal from the town. German forces then pursued the British and their Norwegian allies, who tried to establish new defensive positions further north. The Scots Guards established a position to the north of the Viskisnoia river but were exhausted. When it arrived, the 3rd Independent Company moved to establish defences on a strategic hill but arrived too late as the Germans had already occupied it. The British command now realised that their position was untenable and began a general withdrawal towards the port of Bodö. A delaying position was established at Pothus, some 10 miles from the port, by the 2nd and 3rd Independent Companies, a Norwegian machine gun company and a few 25-pounder guns. Moving up towards them were two battalions of mountain troops, two companies of cyclist troops and a battery of mountain guns. On the night of 25/26 May the Germans crossed a fast-flowing river and outflanked the British/Norwegian positions. By the 25th Lieutenant Colonel Gubbins had been informed that the British were to be evacuated from Bodö. Three Gloster Gladiator fighters stationed at a newly built airstrip at Bodö tried to give support to the British force. They took on a number of Luftwaffe aircraft, shooting down two and damaging another two in one of the few aerial successes for the RAF in Norway. Bodö was bombed on 27 May, destroying the airstrip and other facilities, and killing twelve Norwegian civilians. A fighting withdrawal by the British took place over the next few days. On the night of 29/30 May those British troops who had managed to get to Bodö were evacuated by a force of Royal Navy destroyers. The soldiers of the Norwegian 1st Battalion, 15th Regiment who had covered the withdrawal were evacuated by small boats to the nearby Lofoten Islands. For the Germans their objective of relieving Narvik was made redundant when the port fell temporarily to a combined French and Norwegian force on 28 May.

(**Opposite, above**) Soldiers of the 2nd Gebirgsjager Division rush along a mountain road to go to the aid of their comrades at Narvik. The 3rd Gebirgsjager was in desperate straits and the 2nd had little choice but to try to make the gruelling cross-country march to reinforce them. They were based at the railway junction at Grong and began their march on 5 May, clashing with British troops on the 17th. Before the 2nd Division could reach Narvik the German garrison there had been forced to withdraw by the Allied soldiers besieging the port. (*Author's Collection*)

(**Opposite, below**) Soldiers of the 2nd Gebirgsjager cross a mountain stream during the march from their base at Grong towards their besieged comrades at Narvik. They are travelling light with only minimal equipment but look exhausted by their exertions. Although they were tough troops who were trained to operate in the mountains of Austria, this journey across hostile terrain was to test their endurance to the full. (*Author's Collection*)

Throughout the Norwegian Campaign the Royal Navy, with support from the French Navy, moved men and supplies around the Allied-held ports. The First World War era heavy cruiser HMS *Effingham* was launched in 1917 and underwent several refits before 1940. During the Norwegian Campaign she bombarded German positions and then ferried troops to the port of Bodö on 17 May. The next day she ran aground and began to sink, but not before her entire crew could be offloaded onto other ships. (*Author's Collection*)

This artist's impression from a UK news magazine shows an infantry unit firing from the heights down onto an advancing German armoured column. Such illustrations were used a great deal to show what was happening during the April–May fighting in Norway. In contrast to the dearth of photographs of the campaign in the British press, the Nazi press was filled with images of the German Army, Navy and Air Force. (*Author's Collection*)

Lieutenant General Claude Auchinleck was made commander of the North West Expeditionary Corps in May. Here he is seen on board a ship on his way to Norway with RAF Group Captain Moore perusing a map of the country he was on the way to. His new command was a 'poisoned chalice' and there was little he could do to change the outcome. The failure to turn around the situation in Norway did not affect his career, as the whole army knew that his mission was impossible. *(Author's Collection)*

Two British soldiers taking supplies across a fjord to their unit during the fighting in Nordland in northern Norway in May. This photograph was taken by a soldier who had brought his camera with him to the front line; when he was taken prisoner, the camera was taken away and a German soldier had the film developed. In later life he donated it to a Norwegian archive.
(Arkiv i Nordland, NA143.0134)

(**Above**) Like the previous photograph, this snap was taken by a British soldier who later was taken prisoner in the fighting in Nordland. These troops, wearing part of their winter uniforms, are posing with a friendly Norwegian family. The men from the 24th Guards Brigade wear the new issue fur hat with fold-down ear protection and the standard winter pullover, as well as snow goggles. They were stationed around the town of Mo i Rana, which was to come under attack by the Germans on 17 May. (*Arkiv i Nordland, NA143.0138*)

(**Opposite, above**) Two Norwegian soldiers hunker down behind a snowdrift which provides only minimal cover from the fire of the advancing German troops. During the fighting in Nordland the number of Norwegian units still fighting was reducing as they realised that the war was more or less lost. Many, however, continued to fight beside their British and French allies in the hope that more military assistance would arrive. (*Author's Collection*)

(**Opposite, below**) A lone Norwegian marksman prepares to open fire on German troops advancing towards his position. He is armed with a Norwegian-produced Krag-Jorgensen M1894 rifle, which was based on a US design. Some troops were issued with sniper versions of the rifle but this was not fitted with a telescopic sight but had a heavier barrel. (*Author's Collection*)

(**Above**) Gebirgsjagers – German mountain troops – pose for the cameraman alongside their MG34 light machine gun on its anti-aircraft mount somewhere on the road between the town of Mo i Rana and the Saltdal region of northern Norway. The German advance from central Norway through northern Norway saw limited opposition from the British and Norwegian troops. (*Arkiv i Nordland, NA.0241.0170*)

(**Opposite, above**) A lone German sentry stands guard over drums full of engine oil on a pier at the side of Finneidfjord on 16 May. The fjord was being used for seaplanes to operate from and thus had some strategic importance. Finneidfjord was situated to the north-east of the town of Mosjoen, which had fallen to the Germans on 11 May. (*Author's Collection*)

(**Opposite, below**) These German mountain troops of the 7th Company, 2nd Battalion, 137th Mountain Regiment, 2nd Mountain Division gather around a campfire. They are camped at the village of Krokstrand to the north of the town of Mo i Rana on 17 May. Earlier in the day they had taken part in heavy fighting against British troops who had held the town with orders to stop the German advance. The town's defenders included several companies of Scots Guards and some artillery, including four 25-pounder field guns and some 40mm Bofors guns. For once the British were relatively well armed but they were driven back by the Germans after being outflanked by enemy ski troops. Orders from the new commander of the North Western Expeditionary Force, Lieutenant General Claude Auchinleck, to hold their ground came too late to stop a general retreat. By the 20th the British forces had already withdrawn from the town but were now given orders not to pull back any further. (*Arkiv i Nordland, NA143.0027*)

Men of the 2nd Mountain Division pose in the centre of the town of Mo i Rana after it fell to them. The men of the British garrison holding the town found themselves outflanked by a force of Germans who moved using skis confiscated from the local population. An assault force armed with MP40 submachine guns moved down the Dalselva river and took the defenders by surprise. During the fighting in Nordland the Germans' use of the terrain gave them a great advantage over the British troops, who were stuck to the roads.
(Arkiv i Nordland, NA143.0028)

Gebirgsjagers man an MG34 machine gun on a boat during the German advance through Nordland in mid-May. They would not have been expecting any aerial opposition from the enemy as their Luftwaffe comrades controlled the skies above Norway. They are wearing the standard Wehrmacht overcoat and the field cap with the Edelweiss insignia on the side. (Arkiv i Nordland, NA143.0035)

German soldiers rest at the side of the road near the town of Pothus in the Saltdal valley after the fighting in late May. In the background unescorted British prisoners of war are carrying a wounded comrade to the rear. The fighting that took place on 25 and 26 May was a delaying action by the British Scots Guards and a unit of Norwegians armed with 25-pounder guns. A German force of two battalions of Gebirgsjagers, two companies of cyclist troops and a mountain artillery battery advanced down Saltdal valley. After two days of heavy fighting the Allied troops were told to retire towards the village of Rognan. *(Arkiv i Nordland, NA143.0064)*

From the village of Rognan the retreating British forces were evacuated to the port of Bodö. These two prisoners were captured during the retreat from Rognan, having been left behind by the boats sent to save them. A flotilla of small boats and a ferry transported the British troops to their evacuation port, which came under heavy Luftwaffe attack. They were taken off from the port over three nights from 29 May while a Norwegian battalion held back the advancing Germans. Most Norwegian troops did not know that their allies were being evacuated and when their turn came to escape a company was left behind. *(Arkiv i Nordland, NA143.0049)*

Dejected British soldiers, two of them wounded, are watched over by a German soldier after fighting around the ski resort of Stien on 17 May. The British held defensive positions around Stien, which lay 3 miles south-west of the town of Mo i Rana. When the British withdrew from their positions they left behind much of their equipment and a few troops fell into German hands. (Arkiv i Nordland, NA143.0132)

Another group of prisoners lie exhausted on the grass with their Gebirgsjager captors chatting behind them. The British soldiers fighting in Nordland in mid-May found themselves largely isolated from their command. They did receive orders to continue to fight the German advance but as time went on the one-sided nature of the campaign affected their morale. (Author's Collection)

A Gebirgsjäger MG34 light machine gunner looks down over the rocky terrain at Viskisbrua, close to the Swedish border, on 24 May. By this date the fighting in southern, eastern and central Norway was largely over and the campaign now centred around Narvik. Four days later the vital port fell to French, Polish and Norwegian forces who held it for just eight days. (*Author's Collection*)

A lone German soldier watches for enemy movement from his position close to the Saltdalselva river between the town of Pothus and the village of Rognan. The soldier has camouflaged his M35 helmet with foliage and is armed with a Mauser Kar 98 rifle and an M24 stick grenade. *(Arkiv i Nordland, NA143.0075)*

Gebirgsjagers rest behind a bank giving them cover from British artillery fire, according to the original caption. They were fighting in the vicinity of the Saltdalselva river at the village of Rokland, which is 9 miles south of Rognan. Although the officer is wearing a mountain field cap, his men have donned their M35 steel helmets and are wearing camouflaged ponchos. *(Arkiv i Nordland, NA143.0076)*

Chapter Twelve

The Allied Evacuation from Central Norway

By the last days of April it was obvious that the Allied bases at the ports of Åndalsnes and Namsos were untenable. All the Allied-held ports came under heavy Luftwaffe air attacks throughout the campaign and by this time were in ruins. It had to be acknowledged that the British and French intervention in central Norway had failed and there was little point in continuing the campaign. British troops of the 146th, 148th and 15th Brigades were ordered to head back to the ports they had been landed at for evacuation. It was left to the British commanders to inform their French counterparts that their troops should also head for the ports.

The retreat of Sickle Force from the front line became an ordeal as the 1,800 British soldiers of the 148th Brigade and 300 Norwegian troops struggled to return to their base. They had to travel through horrendous weather, although some were able to use trains. Others had to travel on skis, while the least fortunate had to trudge through snow drifts and along muddy mountain paths. Their withdrawal was covered by the 15th Brigade, fighting alongside their Norwegian allies, who donated four artillery pieces to the mixed force. They managed to hold their positions at Dombås until 30 April, allowing the majority of their comrades to reach their embarkation ports. By the evening of 1 May the troops were boarding ships and the withdrawal had been completed by the early hours of the 2nd. The relieved British prime minister, Neville Chamberlain, informed the House of Commons about the successful evacuation. This was foolish as it alerted the Germans to the evacuation while troops at Namsos were still being evacuated.

The British commander at Namsos, General Carton de Wiart, received orders to prepare for the evacuation of Maurice Force on 27 April. He told his troops in the port to destroy any useful materials to stop them falling into enemy hands. Most of their equipment had already been destroyed by the heavy Luftwaffe raids during the last few weeks. The remnants of the 146th Brigade and the French troops attached to Maurice Force arrived back at the port in the last few days of April. By 3 May the last of the Allied troops had been evacuated, leaving behind Norwegian troops who had covered the withdrawal. Against better judgement, General Carton de Wiart had obeyed orders not to inform the Norwegian commanders of the Allied evacuation.

British soldiers and RAF ground crew take a break in the days before their evacuation from Namsos and Åndalsnes in early May. The evacuation from Åndalsnes was completed by 2 May, and that from Namsos on the following day. A mug of hot sweet tea was an essential prerequisite for the British during the Second World War and in Norway was often accompanied by a hunk of buttered bread. *(Author's Collection)*

Two RAF groundcrew taking a break for a mug of tea, using a packing case as an improvised table. The role of the Royal Air Force during the fighting in Norway was small compared to the role of the Luftwaffe. Unfortunately some of these men and their squadron pilots were to die when HMS *Glorious* was sunk on her doomed journey back to Britain. *(Author's Collection)*

British soldiers bringing skis to be destroyed in the final days of their presence at the port of Namsos. The intention was to destroy anything that could benefit the enemy when they captured Namsos. Most of the Allied troops who took part in the ill-fated Norwegian Campaign were fortunate to return to Britain in early May. Unfortunately they had to abandon the 2,000 Norwegian soldiers who had bravely fought beside them for weeks. It cannot have been easy when they were ordered to leave the port, taking very few Norwegians with them. (Author's Collection)

French troops destroy weapons and equipment in readiness for the evacuation of Namsos in the last days of April. The British commander, General De Wiart, had received orders on 28 April to evacuate Namsos. On the 29th an evacuation convoy was assembled, comprising one French and two Royal Navy destroyers. These three ships were under the command of Lord Louis Mountbatten, who was to rise to much higher things during the Second World War. (Author's Collection)

(**Opposite, above**) A French naval officer carefully makes his way through the ruins of Namsos and heads towards the evacuation centre in the port. For the French in Norway the reality that their country was meanwhile struggling to fight off the German invasion meant their future was uncertain. The evacuation began on 2 May with the Allied ships moving through the fog around the port. (*Author's Collection*)

(**Opposite, below**) A mixed group of Allied personnel gather around a British soldier with a pack of cigarettes in the ruined port of Namsos. Two British soldiers chat with three French Chasseurs D'Alpins and a sailor wearing the distinctive dark blue beret with red pom pom. The French soldiers have fixed white snow covers to their Adrian helmets and the sailor has acquired an army sheepskin coat. (*Author's Collection*)

(**Above**) In a closer image of the previous one, a British sergeant lights the cigarette of a French sailor in an example of 'entente cordial' during the Norwegian Campaign. Both the British and the French were unprepared for the fighting in Norway, showing how difficult it was to resupply an Expeditionary Army by sea. By the time this photograph was taken the French and the British Expeditionary Corps in France were about to face the German offensive on the Western Front. The fighting in Norway became a costly sideshow, whose objectives were no longer vital to the Allied war effort. (*Author's Collection*)

The port of Åndalsnes in flames after one of a number of Luftwaffe raids on the Norwegian port. It was situated to the south of the larger port of Trondheim and was one of several places chosen by the Franco-British commanders to land troops. During the Allied presence there the town came under constant attack by German bombers. When it was decided to terminate the futile campaign in Norway, Åndalsnes was used as an embarkation port from 2 May. (*Author's Collection*)

Major General Sir Bernard Charles Tolver Paget, DSO, MC, was sent to Norway to command the British forces in the Åndalsnes region. His main task was to organise the speedy and safe evacuation of the British forces from Åndalsnes port. The main requirement for British and French officers during the period of evacuation was to maintain a calm atmosphere during the withdrawal from Norway. In recognition of his part in the evacuation Paget was appointed a Companion of the Order of the Bath. (Author's Collection)

On the night of 2/3 May British men wait to board the ship that was to evacuate them from Namsos. This group of soldiers had seen several weeks of action against the advancing German forces. The jumbled equipment they carry indicates the rather disorganised nature of the campaign. Several men are using discarded ski poles as walking aids and may be carrying injuries sustained in the fighting. (Author's Collection)

(**Opposite, above left**) The original caption to this photograph in a German publication says that this 'Tommy' is going back to Britain, but he is in fact a French soldier. Although the entire campaign in Norway was widely regarded as being badly planned, the evacuation of the French and British troops went relatively smoothly. This soldier is taking some of his kit back with him to Britain, where some of the French chose to stay and fight for the Free French. Many others chose to go back to recently defeated France, as they believed that their former Allies, the British, were doomed. (*Author's Collection*)

(**Opposite, above right**) This posed photograph shows Allied troops being evacuated from central Norway in the first days of May. It shows representatives of the three main contingents: (*from left to right*) a French Chasseur D'Alpins, a British soldier and a Norwegian officer. The French soldier and the Norwegian officer are wearing the fur-lined coat favoured by the French Army during the campaign. Presumably the Norwegian has been presented with one of the French coats as a gesture by his allies. (*Author's Collection*)

(**Opposite, below**) French troops appear to make up the majority of these soldiers lying on the decks of a rescue ship sailing from Namsos. The order for the evacuation from Namsos was issued on 27 April and received by the British commander there, General Carton de Wiart, the next day. He informed his French counterpart, General Audet, that all Allied troops should pull back to the port from their forward positions. From 28 April to 2 May a gradual withdrawal was undertaken by French and British units, leaving the Norwegians alone in their positions. (*Author's Collection*)

(**Above**) The French Navy's cruiser *Montcalm* took part in the evacuation of Namsos after replacing another cruiser, the *Emile Bertin*, had been damaged by German air attacks. Although the much larger Royal Navy was responsible for most of the naval actions during the Norwegian Campaign, a substantial number of French ships were also involved. (*Author's Collection*)

The French admiral Cadert peers through his binoculars from the bridge of the troopship *El d'Jezair*. Cadert was in charge of the French contribution to the evacuation of Allied troops from Namsos on 1 May. The admiral had skilfully manoeuvred his ships, *El d'Jezair* and *El Kantara*, into Namsos harbour. His expertise meant that both ships were able to pull up at the stone jetty so that troops could get aboard. His other transport ship, *El Mansour*, stayed a little out to sea and troops were ferried out to her aboard smaller vessels.
(Author's Collection)

HMS *Afridi* was one of sixteen Tribal-class destroyers that were built in 1938 in a last-minute attempt to strengthen the Royal Navy. During the Norwegian Campaign she and her 190-strong crew operated up and down the country's coastline. During the evacuation of Namsos in early May her luck ran out when she was attacked by Stuka dive-bombers on the 3rd. *Afridi* was escorting the heavy cruiser HMS *York* and three French transport ships when she was attacked. She had gone to the aid of a French ship, *Bison*, when she was hit by two bombs. These caused enough damage to sink *Afridi*, with the loss of fifty-two crewmen and thirteen troops who were being evacuated.
(Author's Collection)

At the end of the campaign a number of British and French officers met their men who had been evacuated from Norway on arrival at northern British ports. Here we see the French generals Audet and Mittelhauser, who were accompanied by the British generals Ironside and Carton de Wiart. General Audet had commanded the French forces who fought with the British Army at the port of Namsos. By the time this photograph was taken the more important and disastrous campaign in France was coming to a close. (Author's Collection)

British troops thankful to be back in Britain wave to the press as their transport ship docks in an unspecified northern port on 7 May. The evident relief shown by these men speaks volumes about the confused nature of the fighting in Norway in April and May 1940. After disembarking, these men were addressed by General Edmund Ironside, who told them: 'You did not retreat from Norway. You were ordered out.' (*Author's Collection*)

These British troops have made their journey from Norway to Scotland safely. They have landed at Greenock in Renfrewshire on the west coast, having travelled around the northern tip of Scotland. The journey from Norway was fraught with danger, with Kriegsmarine ships and U-boats lying in wait to attack transport ships like the one seen docked here. *(Author's Collection)*

Chapter Thirteen

The Battle for Narvik, 14 April–28 May

From the German landing at Narvik on 9 April until the end of May the strategic port was fought over. On 14 April the German garrison under the command of General Dietl was made up of 2,000 of his mountain troops. During the siege of Narvik the garrison was reinforced mainly from the air with 1,000 paratroopers. The sinking of the Kriegsmarine destroyers during the sea battles off the port between 10 and 13 April brought Dietl unexpected reinforcements as 2,600 crewmen from the sunk and scuttled destroyers were hastily armed with Norwegian weapons captured from the armoury at Elvegaardsmoen. The sailors were put through some basic infantry training before going to the front to fight alongside the land forces. Another 290 'specialists' were allowed to join the garrison via the Swedish border and during the siege a battalion of paratroopers was flown in.

On 14 April an advance party of two companies of British Scots Guards arrived off Narvik at Harstad on HMS *Southampton*. They joined a naval force under the command of Admiral Lord Cork, who pushed for an immediate attack by 350 Scots Guards and 200 sailors and marines against the port. This was cancelled after objections from the army commander at Narvik, Major General P.J. Macksey. He had made a reconnaissance of the port and decided that a frontal assault on the German defences would destroy his 24th Guards Brigade. Other plans over the next few days were mooted but rejected, and the decision was made for Royal Navy ships to bombard the German garrison into submission. On the 24th a three-hour long bombardment was begun with the guns of a battleship, two cruisers and six destroyers let loose. Dietl expected an infantry assault and was preparing to withdraw his men to the Swedish border but no attack materialised. The Germans were well aware that any assault against the port would have probably succeeded because at this stage in the siege the garrison totalled a single battalion. Macksey, the British commander, now favoured a 'scientific encirclement' followed by an eventual assault. Four battalions of Norwegian troops from the 6th Division under the command of General Fleischer totalling 3,500 men had been put at the Allies' disposal. They were sent to make an all-out assault following the naval bombardment, but the attack resulted in heavy casualties. They lost almost 50 per cent of their men either killed or wounded and had to withdraw to try to recover. Reinforcements that arrived to try to bolster the devastated Norwegians included a small detachment of police, who were intended to keep the peace when the port fell.

On 28 April the 1st Chasseur Light Division under the command of General Marie Emile Bethouart landed at Narvik. As the rest of the division landed, the French vanguard moved up to engage the German defenders. It took until 7 May for the French to complete their landings and they were joined on the 9th by the Polish 'Podhale' Brigade. Units which landed during the eleven-day period included the 27th Chasseur Demi-Brigade, the 13th Foreign Legion Demi-Brigade and the 1st Carpathian Chasseur Demi-Brigades of Polish troops. Although the Poles were described as mountain troops, in reality few of them had experience of this kind of fighting. In total there were four battalions of Poles, two of the Foreign Legion and three battalions of Chasseurs. Fifteen French H35/H39 medium tanks were sent to reinforce the infantry, with twelve actually being landed ready for the assault on Narvik. French 75mm guns and Norwegian field guns were also part of the force besieging Narvik, with the total number of Allied troops now totalling 24,500 men. To counter the several batteries on the Allied side, the Germans had only a single battery of medium mountain guns, which had been flown into the port in Ju 52s.

During the rest of May the battle turned into a siege, with gathering French and Norwegian forces testing the outlying German defences. Allied troops were ordered to destroy railway lines and any form of communication between Narvik and the rest of Norway. The British 24th Guards Brigade was sent south from Harstad to try to stop any relief force from Trondheim reaching the port. General Dietl was increasingly worried about the build-up of Allied troops to the north of Narvik and was reported to be unhappy with the performance of the sailors under his command, and would have been pleased to see the back of them. He was quoted as saying that they were 'useless for combat and a danger to our troops'. Plans were in place to evacuate the destroyer crews anyway as they were needed to perform their naval roles. At this, Dietl did an about-face and told his superiors that the converted sailors were now indispensable for Narvik's defence. On 13 May he told the German high command that he could not hold Narvik for much longer. Plans to fly a parachute battalion to Narvik were put in place but a regiment of mountain troops was prepared instead. On 17 May the 137th Gebirgsjager Regiment was parachuted into Narvik after receiving a paratroopers' crash course. Regardless of these reinforcements Dietl knew that he was only fighting for time and that he might have to evacuate the port.

The Allied forces surrounding the port were now Norwegian and French, with the former holding positions to the north of Narvik. To the south were three Polish battalions that had replaced British and French troops, and pressure was now being applied on the German defences from two directions. On the 21st Dietl shortened his lines of defence by withdrawing units from the northern front. He was now faced by a lack of morale amongst his disgruntled garrison, with some even refusing to move their positions as they had been ordered. In a bit of an anti-climax the French and Norwegian troops took Narvik on 28 May. Royal Navy ships landed French Chasseurs D'Alpins and a handful of H39 tanks on the beaches of Narvik. Despite repeated Luftwaffe bombing raids on the attacking forces, they made progress against heavy German fire. The assault force was made up of two battalions of Foreign Legionnaires, the Polish 'Podhale' Brigade and the Norwegian 8th Brigade. In support were two battalions of Chasseurs D'Alpins and a bombardment from three Royal Navy cruisers and five destroyers. Dietl's troops made an orderly withdrawal up the iron ore railway towards the town of Bjornfjell on the Swedish border. They established a defence line around the town but did not have long to wait before they could retake Narvik. The Norwegians were allowed the honour of entering the deserted port first at 17.00 and were followed in by their French Allies. A harsh reality was that the capture of Narvik did not really change the general situation in Norway. Within a few days the orderly evacuation of the port began, with the first French troops leaving on 4 June.

General Dietl, the popular commander of the 3rd Gebirgs Division, inspects some of his mountain troops at Narvik. The 50-year-old general was an ardent Nazi, having been involved with the National Socialists since the 1920s. After the campaign in Norway he was given command of the German Lapland Army (AOK Lappland). This army, raised in 1942, was responsible for the control of northern Norway and Finland and was renamed the 20th Mountain Army. Dietl was killed in June 1944 when a Junkers 52 transport plane went down in Styria in Austria. (Author's Collection)

A Luftwaffe corporal sits on the quay at Narvik during the German occupation of the port in April 1940. He has been issued with snow goggles which he wears on the standard side cap of the German Air Force. The role of the 10th Air Corps during the campaign was vital to the eventual German victory in June 1940. Some 500 German transport planes flew 30,000 troops into Norway during the fighting in what was the first major airlift in history. (Author's Collection)

(**Opposite, above left**) A Kriegsmarine sailor who is fighting on land during the Narvik campaign pictured in discussion with General Dietl, the commander of the 3rd Gerbirgs Division. Dietl was not impressed by the performance of many of his naval personnel, whom he disparaged on several occasions. Although he was relieved to expand his garrison with these redundant sailors, they were not ground troops. He tried to use them to fill the gaps left in Narvik's perimeter, but they were not trained as infantry. (Author's Collection)

(**Opposite, below**) The crews of the nine Kriegsmarine destroyers sunk or put out of action during the second battle of Narvik were quickly redeployed as ad-hoc infantry. Most of these naval personnel were used to guard the shoreline of the fjord against Allied assaults. They were mostly armed with 'war-booty' Norwegian rifles and other weaponry and were also equipped with brown leather belts and ammunition pouches. These men appear to be armed with standard German Army Mauser 98K rifles taken from their ships' armouries. (Author's Collection)

(**Opposite, above right**) This Kriegsmarine sailor is fighting around the port of Narvik as an infantryman after his ship was put out of action by the Royal Navy. Most sailors had to be armed with rifles captured from Norwegian stores during the first days of the campaign. Some 8,000 Krag-Jorgensen M1894 rifles were taken from abandoned Norwegian Army stores. Besides his sailor's hat, he is wearing a woollen service tunic of the type issued to ships' crews for winter duties ashore. (Author's Collection)

The original caption to this photograph reads: 'A new replacement had arrived, in the background a stone monument for the Ofoten Railway.' All the mountain troops are wearing the standard woollen uniform with the mountain ski cap. During the battle for Narvik the German garrison had little heavy equipment and only a few mountain guns available. (*Author's Collection*)

(**Opposite, above left**) German paratroopers (*Fallschirmjager*) of the 7th Air Division gather in the centre of Narvik before moving to their defensive positions. The 1,000 paratrooper reinforcements who were dropped over Bjornfjell by Junkers 52 transport planes greatly bolstered Narvik's defences. At this stage in the war these elite troops had yet not proved themselves but they would soon do so during the conquest of the Netherlands. (*Author's Collection*)

(**Opposite, above right**) These paratroopers are preparing to be dropped over Narvik on 14 May to reinforce the garrison there. The first contingent amounted to only sixty-six men but their arrival was welcomed by their comrades. They were to be joined over the next few weeks by a more substantial number of paratroopers and other troops. (*Author's Collection*)

(**Opposite, below**) This *Fallschirmjager* jumping from a Junkers Ju 52/3m transport plane is part of the reinforcement battalion dropped over Narvik. In total, 1,050 paratroopers and mountain troops arrived to bolster the besieged garrison in May 1940. Another 160 'specialists' reached Narvik via the Swedish border in preparation for the coming Allied assault on the port. In desperation the Germans gave two companies of mountain troops a truncated paratroop training course and dropped them into Narvik. (*Author's Collection*)

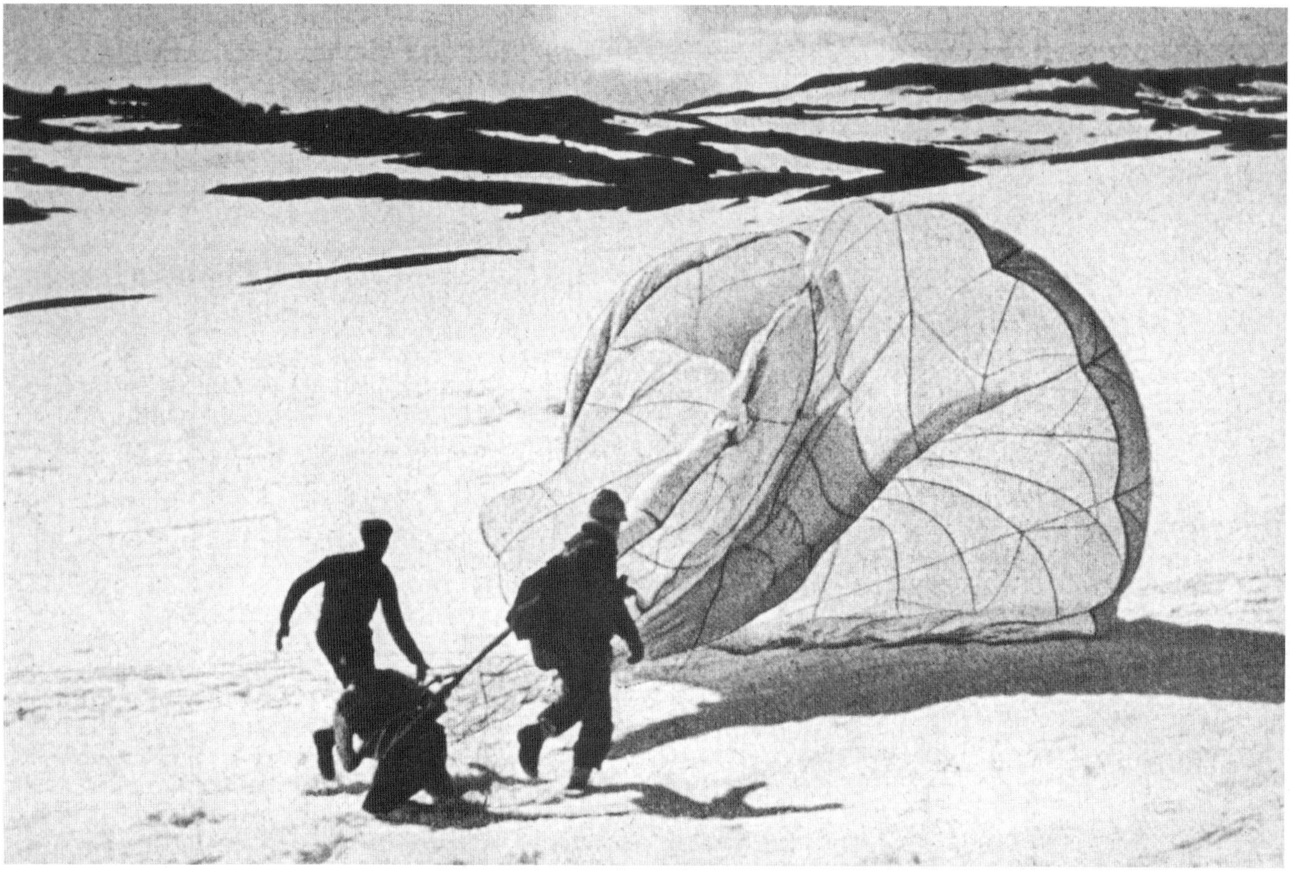

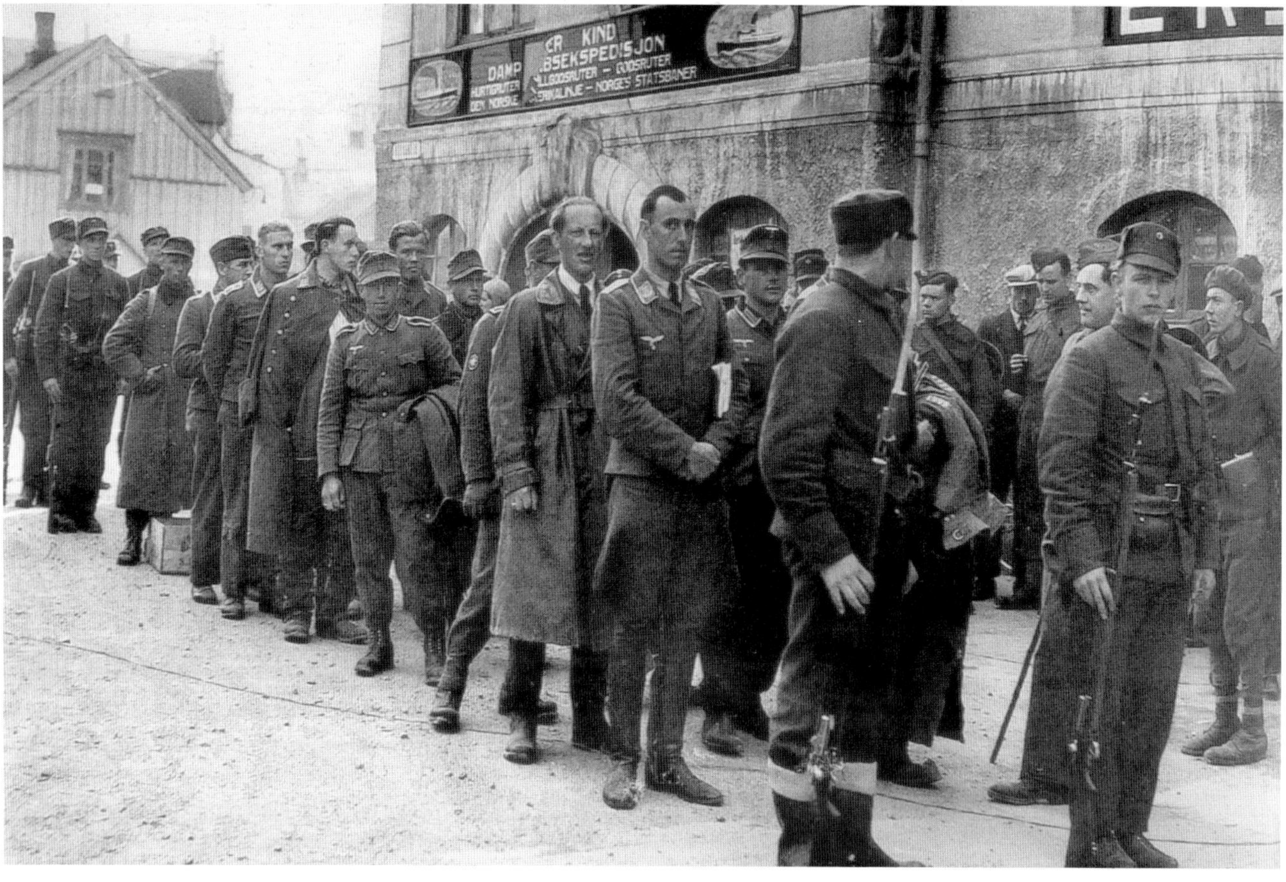
KIND
DAMP
HURTIGRUTER
DEN NORSKE
GODSRUTER
NORGES STATSBANER

(**Opposite, above**) German paratroopers were dropped as reinforcements for the isolated garrison at Narvik. The 7th Parachute Division took part in a number of operations during the Norwegian Campaign. Paratroopers landed to the east of the port and joined the garrison, which eventually reached a strength of 5,600 made up of mountain troops, paratroopers and sailors fighting as infantry. (*Author's Collection*)

(**Opposite, below**) A group of Luftwaffe and Wehrmacht personnel being held by Norwegian troops at Harstad, the British headquarters 35 miles from Narvik. Harstad was on the island of Hinnoy and to reach Narvik by ship involved sailing through a number of narrow sea passages, then navigating south through Vaagsfjord and then east through Ofotfjord before entering Herjangsfjord, on the south shore of which Narvik was situated. (*Author's Collection*)

(**Above**) British 3.7-inch anti-aircraft guns in their positions close to Narvik. On 6 May eight of these guns arrived at Harstad and were used throughout the battle to fend off the regular Luftwaffe attacks. The crewmen wear their British Mk I steel helmets along with their sheepskin-lined brown leather jerkins. These modern guns were part of the small amount of Allied heavy weaponry that was landed in Norway. (*Author's Collection*)

A Bofors anti-aircraft crew prepare to defend the port of Namsos which, like Åndalsnes, another port in Allied hands, was constantly bombed by the Luftwaffe. The ships at anchor in the Allied-held ports had insufficient anti-aircraft armament so the German bombers faced little opposition. Constant German air raids on the two ports meant that they were largely unusable by the transport ships that it was hoped would bring reinforcements and supplies to the Allies. (Author's Collection)

Chasseurs D'Alpins pose aboard their transport ship on the way to Norway with their 81mm Brandt medium mortar. These troops are kitted out with the best available winter clothing that the French Army had to offer. Their sheepskin coats have been issued to supplement their standard woollen uniforms and several of the men are wearing snow goggles. (Author's Collection)

Apprehensive Polish troops aboard a transport ship as they are taken to Narvik in early May. The 1st and 2nd Demi-Brigades of the Polish contingent arrived at the port in the first days of the month. Troops of the 2nd Polish Battalion were sent to relieve the French forces at Bjerkvik, arriving after a gruelling 15mile march on 15 May. They arrived too late to take part in the fighting there and instead were sent to relieve the 2nd Battalion, South Wales Borderers on the Ankenes peninsula. (Author's Collection)

Two Polish signallers pictured in the hills around Narvik during the build-up to the Allied attack on the port. The Polish Brigade held positions to the south-west of Narvik on the Ankenes peninsula, from where they faced the German defenders. Most of the German defence forces in late May were not in the port itself but at Bjornfjell, from where they proceeded to destroy the infrastructure at Narvik. (Author's Collection)

During the battles around Narvik the Polish-held positions on the Ankenes peninsula were constantly threatened by German troops there. Savage skirmishes took place between the Poles and their bitter enemies in the barren terrain of the peninsula. These men have created a small shelter at their hilltop position and keep a keen eye out for any German movements. *(Author's Collection)*

The light machine gun crew of a Chasseurs d'Alpins unit have established a position on the heights above Ramboks Fjord. This narrow channel of water separated the French lines from Narvik during the early fighting around the port. They are armed with MAS 36 rifles, while the machine gun is a Chatelleraut M1924, the most modern type in service with the French Army in 1940. *(Author's Collection)*

French Legionnaires of the 13th Light Mountain Demi-Brigade of the Foreign Legion advance across a railway on the outskirts of Narvik. The 13th Demi-Brigade was made up of two Legionnaire battalions and saw its first action at Bjerkvik, to the north of the port, on 13 May. These men fought well during the early battle for Narvik, taking four objectives and capturing enemy equipment including ten Junkers 52 transport planes that were stuck on an icy lake. (Author's Collection)

Norwegian and French ski troops seen on patrol on the Narvik front in May. This example of good co-operation between the Allies took place during the battle for Narvik, where the Allied and Norwegian units worked well together. Norwegian children grew up learning how to ski, as did French children born in the Alpine regions of their country. Note that the French troops carry their skis crossed behind their backs, while the Norwegian carry theirs over their shoulders. (Getty Images)

(**Opposite, above left**) Two officers of a Tronderbattalion stand outside their headquarters in the north of Norway. Their 750-strong unit, raised in the border region in north Norway, had served along the Norway-USSR border during the Winter War and when the Germans invaded they were moved to the south of Tromsø. They took up positions at Lavangen, north-east of Narvik, on 17 April and were designated as the 1st Battalion, 12th Infantry Regiment. They were operating in extreme temperatures and their number had already been reduced to 643 men when they came under attack by a smaller but better armed German force on 24 May, with both sides suffering heavy casualties. During the battle 34 Norwegians were killed, 61 wounded and 174 captured, while the Germans lost 7 dead and 14 wounded. (*Trondheim Byarchiv*)

(**Opposite, below**) A patrol of mountain troops moving off into the snow-covered hills above Narvik. The troops are carrying full kit as they prepare to take up positions on the mountains overlooking the port. It was difficult for the German garrison to protect the entire perimeter of Narvik and the defenders' positions were often widely dispersed. With only 5,600 men at his disposal, General Dietl had to use his available forces to the full. (*Author's Collection*)

(**Opposite, above right**) Mountain troops of the 3rd Gerbirgs Division move up into the hills above Narvik. The struggle for the port was to see troops fighting in various conditions which were often difficult. These elite soldiers are well equipped for the campaign with mountain boots, snow goggles and, of course, their skis. (*Author's Collection*)

(**Above**) The only type of artillery that the Narvik garrison had was the 7.5cm leichtes Gerbirgsgeschutz 36 mountain gun, seen here in action. A four-gun battery was flown into the besieged town and went into action against the Norwegian and French field guns of the Allied forces. Unfortunately the original caption to this photograph does not categorically say that it is one of the mountain guns used at Narvik. (*Author's Collection*)

The Gebirgsjager crew of an MG34 light machine gun scan the skies in case any stray RAF aircraft might attack them. As the garrison of Narvik withdrew towards the Swedish border, they might have expected that the Allied ground forces who had captured the port would have air support. Although additional RAF planes had been brought into Norway during the campaign, they had little effect on the fighting. (Author's Collection)

(**Opposite, above**) Royal Navy ships shelling dug-in German positions at Bjerkvik in support of French landings at Narvik on the night of 12/13 May. The change in tactics by the Allies to shift their campaigning from central Norway to the north meant a series of evacuations and landings in May. Within days the French would be fighting the German defenders of Narvik on a number of fronts. (Author's Collection)

(**Opposite, below**) A Norwegian heavy machine gun crew fire their weapon in fighting to the north of Narvik during May. They are firing their Colt Mitraljose m/29 at a low-flying aircraft that was supporting the Narvik garrison. These guns fired a type of ammunition – 7.92mm x 61mm – that was not used in any other weapon. On top of the gun barrel is a primitive anti-aircraft sight, which appears to have been a fixture of many of these guns. (Author's Collection)

(**Opposite, above**) Norwegian cavalrymen patrolling the outskirts of Narvik on local fjord ponies, a breed native to the country. The main Norwegian units were stationed to the north-west of the port, while most French troops were dug-in to the north-east. Hitler was worried by the build-up of Norwegian, British, French and Polish troops around Narvik and had suggested that the German garrison should withdraw from the port into neutral Sweden. However, the German commander, General Dietl, was determined to hold out with his garrison of mountain troops, sailors and paratroops. (*Author's Collection*)

(**Opposite, below**) The crew of a Norwegian Army 7.5cm M/01 field gun with a modified gun carriage firing at German positions during the fighting north of Narvik in May 1940. Although the number of Norwegians fighting alongside the Franco-British reduced as the campaign went on, some stayed loyal to the end. One problem for the Norwegians was that their units had been dispersed and armouries containing more shells had been captured by the Germans. (*Author's Collection*)

(**Above, left**) Again illustrating the cooperation between the various Allied contingents fighting at Narvik, here a British soldier helps his Norwegian ally to arrange his kit before going out on patrol. The 6th Norwegian Division reached a strength of almost 10,000 men during the campaign. Along with the French, British and Polish contingents, there were a total of 24,500 troops fighting the Germans. (*Author's Collection*)

(**Above, right**) Two Norwegian soldiers of the 6th Division rolling cigarettes during a break from the fighting around Narvik. The soldiers wear the M1934 uniform with the M1931 Baltic helmet and have snow coveralls over their tunics and on their headgear. Under the command of General Carl Gustav Fleischer, the 6th Division was battle ready on 9 April. It was one of the few Norwegian units that was prepared for the coming campaign, largely due to it being stationed close to the border with Finland. (*Author's Collection*)

These two Norwegians fighting alongside the French to capture Narvik appear to be civilian volunteers. The man on the left is armed with his own hunting rifle and his colleague may also have his own weapon. These men have used the German parachutes left on the ground to produce snow suits to wear over their civilian clothing. Such men would continue the war against the Germans as resistance fighters until 1945. (*Author's Collection*)

(**Opposite, above**) Gebirgsjagers move along the shore of a fjord close to Narvik during the battle for the Norwegian port. They had to rely on rubber dinghies that they had brought with them from Germany to move from position to position during the fighting. When local rowing boats were available they were, of course, used but the Norwegians tried to hide them whenever possible. (*Author's Collection*)

(**Opposite, below left**) A rather forlorn-looking Luftwaffe pilot is watched over by French guards, having crashed behind Franco-British lines near Narvik. The Luftwaffe largely dominated the skies over Norway but a number of their aircraft were shot down by the RAF. Whether this pilot was taken back to Britain as a prisoner when the Allies withdrew in May 1940 or was released is not known. (*Author's Collection*)

(**Opposite, below right**) General Fleischer, the commander of the 6th Norwegian Division, smokes his pipe in pensive mood during a break from the fighting for Narvik. Fleischer, like General Ruge, was determined to resist the German invasion and had the best equipped division under his command. His men fought in northern Norway and along with British, French and Polish troops took Narvik from the Germans on 28 May. (*Author's Collection*)

The wreckage of a Heinkel 111 bomber shot down over Narvik during the heavy fighting for the port lies on a bleak hillside above the port. Luftwaffe bombers did not face much aerial opposition but as the campaign progressed a number of British medium and heavy anti-aircraft guns were landed at nearby Harstad. Poor weather conditions over Norway also adversely affected the German aircraft, with a number lost for this reason. (*Author's Collection*)

In the early morning light of 27 May a patrol of the Norwegian 6th Division moves through the hills above Narvik. The Norwegians made up a substantial contingent of the force besieging the port and were given the honour of entering the town first when it fell later that day. They are wearing white snow suits over their grey woollen uniforms and are still armed with the Krag-Jorgensen M1894. Ammunition for these rifles was running low as the armouries that held them had nearly all fallen into German hands. (*Norsk Telegrambyraa*)

This machine gun position on the outskirts of Narvik is manned by German troops fighting in freezing conditions. They are using one of the 315 captured Norwegian machine guns, with this one being a Colt-Browning M29 model. By 21 May the morale of the German garrison was declining and the soldiers were exhausted. There were many instances of soldiers falling asleep in their machine gun positions when they should have been alert for an attack. *(Author's Collection)*

HMS *Curlew*, a C-class anti-aircraft cruiser, was operating in northern Norwegian waters during the closing stages of the Battle for Narvik, providing anti-aircraft cover for the many ships bringing supplies to the Allied troops besieging the port. She was stationed off Narvik on 26 May when she was spotted by a group of Junkers Ju 88 medium bombers of the Kampfgeschwader 30. They bombed the cruiser, and she sank in Lavangsfjord, Ofotfjord. The majority of the 460-strong crew were thankfully saved from the sea but nine men were drowned. *(Author's Collection)*

The French armoured contingent in Norway was formed from the Compagnie Autonome de Chars de Combat – the Independent Tank Company. This company had been created to help in a possible intervention on the Finnish side during the Winter War. All its fifteen tanks were H39 medium tanks with the shorter gun than was usually fitted to this model. Having been landed at Narvik on 7 May, the surviving twelve tanks took part in the fighting around the port until they were withdrawn on 8 June. This tank, pictured on the perimeter of Narvik, is surrounded by the debris of war and it looks like branches have been laid to enable it to advance. (Author's Collection)

When Narvik fell to the Norwegian and French assaults on 28 May, they took 400 German prisoners. Here a platoon of French Legionnaires have taken a group of Germans prisoner, with one being offered a cigarette by his captor. An elderly civilian looks on with interest.
(Author's Collection)

British troops investigate a French H39 tank in a village near Narvik in the aftermath of taking the port on 28 May. The French Foreign Legion had managed to land five of these infantry tanks in what was the first sea landing of such vehicles in history. This group of Allied soldiers appear to have been picked to show the cosmopolitan nature of the force besieging the port. They include several British soldiers, a member of the Polish Brigade and a few Chasseurs D'Alpins. (*Author's Collection*)

In the closing stages of the battle for Narvik, a pair of transport ships moving past the port come under fire from Luftwaffe bombers. Throughout the majority of the siege of Narvik the Royal Navy ruled the waves, with the Kriegsmarine having been defeated by 13 April. To balance the situation, the German Air Force ruled the skies over Norway, inflicting damage on a number of Allied ships during the battle. (*Author's Collection*)

German paratroopers march into Narvik after the withdrawal of the Allied troops from the port. The Allies had withdrawn by 7 June and the Germans were able to move into the city without opposition. When they reached the port they were disappointed to find that the Allies had demolished most of its facilities. (*Author's Collection*)

Chapter Fourteen

The End of the Norwegian Campaign

The evacuation of the last Allied forces from Narvik in early June left the remaining Norwegian units to fend for themselves. In addition to seeing the departure of their 'saviours' from Britain and France, there was bad news from the Western Front. France was on the verge of defeat after the stupendous success of the German Blitzkrieg and any slim hope of further assistance for Norway was now gone. Those Norwegian units that were still fighting were cut off from one another and did not receive any orders from their commander, General Ruge. He was unable to contact most of his widely dispersed units and it was now up to units or individuals who wanted to keep fighting to get out of Norway. There were still 4,000 troops who had been attached to General Paget's command. Other units of a few hundred or thousand men were still in the field in the vicinity of Namsos. By 7 June, when the last Allied troops were evacuated from Narvik, the Germans had defeated the French. The British Expeditionary Force had been evacuated from Dunkirk, and Britain was now fighting the Germans alone. On 6 June the last large formation of Norwegian troops, the 6th Division, laid down their arms and the campaign in Norway was over.

The failure of the Allied land campaign was soon to be followed by another disaster, this time at sea. After the grievous losses suffered by the Kriegsmarine in early April, the Germans wanted to score a decisive victory of their own. A plan was conceived by the German naval command on 14 May to send a strong force to Norway with the aim of disrupting the Royal Navy's operations along the coast. It would take more than two weeks for these plans to be enacted while the Kriegsmarine waited for some of its ships to be repaired. The new Naval Group West was put under the command of Vice Admiral Marschall and was made up of two battlecruisers, *Scharnhorst* and *Gneisenau*, and the heavy cruiser *Admiral Hipper*. These three ships had been undergoing emergency repairs to damage sustained in the naval engagements off Norway in the opening days of the campaign. Escorted by four destroyers, they left Kiel on 4 June and headed north-westwards towards Norway. Marschall's orders were to attack any Franco-British shipping off the coast of Norway, and his ships were to enter Andfiord and Vaagsfiord where he expected to find enemy ships. His intelligence told him that he could expect to come across one or two Royal Navy battleships close to the coast and an aircraft carrier which had been sighted 200 miles out to sea. On 8 June, as the Allied evacuation came to an end, the aircraft-carrier HMS *Glorious* and its escorting destroyers, HMS *Acasta* and HMS *Ardent*, were sailing back to Britain when they ran into the *Scharnhorst* and *Gneisenau* heading for Harstad. With their 11-inch guns, they totally outgunned the Royal Navy ships and all three were soon sunk, taking almost every crew member with them. Before she sank HMS *Acasta* managed to fire a torpedo at *Scharnhorst*, causing damage. Although the loss of the three ships was a tragedy for the Royal Navy, it did not really affect the situation off Norway and the Kriegsmarine was still at a disadvantage, having lost so many of its ships in April.

(**Right**) Two older officers, one from the German Gebirgsjagers and the other from the Norwegian Army, are pictured here shaking hands. Although some Norwegian units gave up in early April without resistance, most did fight for a while. The units that were isolated in the south and east of Norway had little choice but to surrender as their prospects of receiving supplies and military support were minimal. (*Author's Collection*)

(**Opposite, above**) Norwegian soldiers are seen towards the end of the fighting as they move to fight the Germans in central Norway. After the British and French withdrew from central Norway at the start of May, some Norwegian units continued to fight. Their comrades from the 6th Division were still fighting around Narvik until the end of May. (*Author's Collection*)

(**Opposite, below**) Newly captured Norwegian soldiers read a German newssheet given to them by their captors in late May. Many Norwegian units which had continued fighting after 9 April were isolated from one another. Although they were supposed to be operating under the orders of their high command and General Ruge, communications were a major problem. Such units often had to operate independently, with only the most determined continuing to fight the invaders until the end of the campaign. (*Author's Collection*)

The Norwegian commander-in-chief Major General Otto Ruge, pictured at his headquarters on 7 June 1940. He had refused to leave Norway along with the King and his government as he would not abandon his soldiers. Ruge was angry at the abandonment of his army by the Allies but in reality there was little that could be done. This was especially the case as the British and French armies were on the verge of defeat in the fighting on the Western Front. (*Author's Collection*)

(**Opposite, above**) Norwegian civilians make their way to the northern border with Sweden as the Allies face defeat. In the first two years of the German Occupation, the Swedish authorities decided to send back large numbers of Norwegian refugees. The Swedes were worried about the effect on the German observance of their neutrality if they allowed too many Norwegians to seek refuge. Local Swedish officials did allow some Norwegians to be transferred to transit camps and the rules were relaxed from 1942. (*Author's Collection*)

(**Opposite, below**) Norwegian civilians and military personnel pictured at the Swedish border ready to cross into the neutral country in June 1940. A large number of Norwegians crossed the border in the immediate wake of the campaign. During the remainder of the Second World War an estimated 50,000 Norwegians fled to Sweden. Political activists, resistance fighters and Jews fled for their lives during the Occupation. (*Author's Collection*)

(**Above**) Anti-aircraft gunners on the Kriegsmarine cruiser *Admiral Hipper* firing their guns in Norwegian waters in June 1940. *Admiral Hipper* was part of Admiral Wilhelm Marschall's task force sent in early June to attack Allied shipping at the British-held port of Harstad. When his ships sailed from Kiel naval base on 4 June Marschall was unaware that the Allies were already evacuating the ports they held in Norway. (*Author's Collection*)

(**Opposite, above**) The Kriegsmarine battlecruiser *Gneisenau* in harbour in Germany before sailing with Admiral Marschall's task force. Along with her sister ship *Scharnhorst*, she was to form the task force's cutting edge during Operation Juno. *Gneisenau* and *Scharnhorst* had the same armament, with nine 11-inch, twelve 5.9-inch and fourteen 4.1-inch guns, as well as sixteen 3.7-inch and sixteen 0.79-inch anti-aircraft guns. Both also had six torpedo tubes installed. For reconnaissance at sea each carried three Arado 196A seaplanes, which were armed with machine guns and could carry a single 110lb bomb under each wing. (*Author's Collection*)

(**Opposite, below**) *Scharnhorst* (seen here) and her sister ship *Gneisenau* had the same displacement of 32,100 tons. When *Scharnhorst* opened fire on HMS *Glorious* she achieved the distinction of the world's furthest recorded naval warfare hit on the doomed Royal Navy ship. (*Author's Collection*)

HMS *Ardent* and HMS *Acasta* were given the task of protecting the ageing aircraft-carrier HMS *Glorious*. *Ardent* was built in the 1920s and launched in 1929, and was one of eight A-class destroyers in the Royal Navy. She had taken part in the landing of Allied troops at Narvik in mid-April and at Bodö later in the month. After returning to the UK for repairs she was one of five destroyers sent to escort two Royal Navy aircraft-carriers, HMS *Glorious* and HMS *Ark Royal*, to Norway. *Ardent* remained off Norway to provide escort duties for *Glorious*, and was joined by HMS *Acasta*. Her crew were to sacrifice themselves in a futile battle with a superior German force on 8 June. A handful of crewmen from the two ships were saved but several died of wounds and only two sailors survived to be taken into captivity. From the combined crews of 337 men, only Able Seaman Cyril Carter of *Acasta* and Able Seaman Roger Hook of *Ardent* survived. (Author's Collection)

HMS *Acasta*, seen here before the war, had a displacement of 1,350 tons and was armed with four 4.7-inch guns. Along with her sister destroyer HMS *Ardent*, she was tasked with providing an escort for the aircraft-carrier HMS *Glorious* in early June. Her crew fought bravely in a one-sided battle with the powerful Kriegsmarine force sailing towards Norway. When the two German battlecruisers opened fire on HMS *Glorious* from 28,000 yards, the destroyers tried to protect her. HMS *Acasta* and HMS *Ardent* valiantly turned towards the German ships but the battle was always going to be a short and one-sided affair. *Acasta* did manage to hit *Scharnhorst* with a torpedo but both Royal Navy ships were soon sunk. (Author's Collection)

The converted aircraft-carrier HMS Glorious pictured at the start of the war a few months before her tragic sinking on 8 June. From her original incarnation as a battlecruiser built in 1915, she had been rebuilt in the 1920s as an aircraft-carrier. In late 1939 Glorious was tasked with searching for the German cruiser Graf Spee in the Indian Ocean. Two fighter squadrons were evacuated by her from Norway, with ten Gloster Gladiators as well as a few Hurricanes landing on her in a risky operation. The tragedy of the ship's sinking was exacerbated by the fact that these planes and their crews were lost when she sank. (Author's Collection)

The British troopship SS Orama sinking after being shelled by the combined German naval force of Admiral Hipper, Scharnhorst and Gneisenau. On 8 June she was 300 miles off the northern Norwegian coast transporting British troops from Narvik when she was hit and sank with the loss of nineteen men. Another 280 men were saved by the Royal Navy destroyers that were escorting the larger troopships. Some were also saved by Admiral Hipper, whose crew searched for survivors, as was often the practice in naval warfare. (Author's Collection)

At the end of the Norwegian Campaign this crewman of a Flak 30 20mm anti-aircraft gun scans the horizon for any enemy activity. Nazi Germany's control of Norway gave the Kriegsmarine a great advantage in its attempts to intercept the Arctic convoys heading to the Soviet Union. However, the loss of a large proportion of its surface fleet during the Norwegian Campaign meant that the battle in the North Atlantic would be largely fought by Germany's U-boat fleet. (*Author's Collection*)